THE

UNERRING FORTUNE-TELLER:

CONTAINING THE CELEBRATED

ORACLE OF HUMAN DESTINY,

OR

BOOK OF FATE:

BEING

AN ACCURATE INTERPRETER OF THE MYSTICAL SIGNS
AND HEAVENLY BODIES;

ALSO EMBRACING THE FRENCH, ITALIAN, AND ENGLISH METHODS OF
TELLING FORTUNES WITH CARDS, AND A NEW AND ENTER-
TAINING PROCESS OF FORTUNE-TELLING WITH DICE.

ALSO CONTAINING SEVENTY-NINE GOOD AND BAD OMENS, WITH THEIR INTER
PRETATIONS, ONE HUNDRED AND EIGHTY-SEVEN WEATHER OMENS, AND

NAPOLEON'S ORACULUM.

BY MADAME LE NORMAND,

FORTUNE-TELLER TO THE EMPEROR NAPOLEON.

4880 Lower Valley Road, Atglen, Pennsylvania 19301

CONTENTS.

	PAGE
THE ORACLE OF HUMAN DESTINY	3
Directions for Consultation, &c.	3
The Fortunate Day	4
Table of the Cœlestial Signs which Influence the Destinies of Men	6
Corresponding Questions, which are to be put to THE ORACLE	7
Answers of THE ORACLE	8
FORTUNE-TELLING BY CARDS	61
SIGNIFICATION OF THE CARDS	61
The Eight Clubs	61
The Eight Hearts	62
The Eight Diamonds	62
The Eight Spades	63
SIGNIFICATION OF DIFFERENT CARDS OF THE SAME DENOMINATION	63
HOW TO READ THE EVENTS, PAST AND TO COME	64
No. 1. Dealing the Cards by Threes	64
No. 2. Dealing the Cards by Sevens	67
No. 3. Dealing the Cards by Fifteens	68
No. 4. The Twenty-one Cards	70
THE ITALIAN METHOD	71
PRESENT, PAST, AND FUTURE	73
THE STAR METHOD OF CONSULTING THE CARDS	75
To know if you will get your Wish	77
THE ENGLISH METHOD OF CONSULTING THE CARDS	77
To tell whether you will get your Wish	79
FORTUNE-TELLING WITH DICE	79
Table of Questions	79
Table of Answers	80
GOOD AND BAD OMENS WITH THEIR INTERPRETATIONS	101
Good and Evil Days	103
The Month of May	104
Friday	105
Hours in the Day fatal to Life	105
Nail Gifts.—Sneezing	106
Love-Knots	106
Spiders	107, 110, 112
Throwing an old Shoe	107
The Horse-Shoe Charm	107

	PAGE
Cauls	108
Spilling Salt	108
Putting on Shoes and Stockings	108
To Arise on the Right Side	109
Nose, Omens respecting	109
Biting of Fleas	109
Washing the Hands	109
Candle Omens	109
Letters, Omens respecting	109
Spoons.—Pictures.—Rings	110
Miscellaneous Omens	110–119
Killing Certain Birds, &c	111
Owls.—Animals Crossing your Path	111
Garters	112
Crickets.—The Death-Watch	113
Looking-Glasses	114
Thirteen Persons at Table	115
Dogs	115
Odd Numbers	116
Knives and Scissors	117
Stumbling while going up Stairs	118
Concluding Remarks	119
ONE HUNDRED AND EIGHTY-SEVEN WEATHER OMENS	119
For Fine and Dry Weather of Long Continuance	119
For Fine Weather of Shorter Duration	120
For Continued Rainy and Showery Weather	121
For Foul and Wet Weather	121
For Storm	124
For Increase of Storm	125
For Decrease of Storm	125
For Thunder and Heavy Rain	125
For the Approach of Thunder	126
For Continued Thunder Showers	126
Abatement of Thunder Storms	126
For Colder Weather	126
For Increase of Warmth or Heat	126
For Frost	126
For Thaw	127
Miscellaneous	127
HYMEN'S LOTTERY	128
NAPOLEON'S ORACULUM; OR, BOOK OF FATE	128
How to Work the ORACULUM	129
To Obtain the Answer	129
ORACULUM	130
Tables of Answers	131

Entered according to Act of Congress, in the year 1866, by
DICK & FITZGERALD,
In the Clerk's Office of the District Court of the United States for the Southern District of New York.

THE ORACLE OF HUMAN DESTINY

DIRECTIONS FOR CONSULTATION, ETC.

IN order to consult the ORACLE, with advantage, the Inquirer, must state the nature of his Question to any Lady in the company, who shall act as Priestess for the time being. The Priestess having inspected the Table of Cœlestial Signs, shall now point out to the Inquirer which of the whole Twelve exercises an influence, or presides over the subject under consideration. The Inquirer shall then write out, on a slip of paper, the Question, which is placed opposite to it—that being the form in which it must be put to the ORACLE.

These preliminaries being duly arranged, the Priestess must shuffle a pack of common Playing-Cards,* and, having placed them on the table, the Inquirer is to *cut* them. The bottom Card of the division

---

* Cards were originally invented in Egypt; though the current opinion of the present day is, that they were invented about a century or two back, and first used for the amusement of a young French prince. That Cards, however, are of the high origin above asserted, is easily proved by their numbers, suites, and characters, corresponding strictly with the astronomical signs and calculations of the ancient Egyptians, who are acknowledged to have been better acquainted with the motions of the heavenly bodies than any other nation that ever existed. But to the proof:—

The *Colors* are *two*, Red and Black, answering to the *two Equinoxes*.

The *Suites* are *four*, answering to the *four Seasons*. The emblems of these formerly were, and still are in Spain: for the *Heart*, a *Cup*, which is emblematic of *Winter*; for the *Spade* an *Acorn*, the emblem of *Autumn*; for the *Club* a *Trefoil*, the emblem of *Summer*; and for the *Diamond* a *Rose*, which is the emblem of *Spring*

The *twelve Court Cards* answer to the *twelve Months*; and these were formerly painted with the *Signs of the Zodiac*.

The *fifty-two Cards*, or whole *Pack*, answer to the number of *Weeks* in the *Year*.

The *thirteen Cards* in each *Suite* answer to the number of *Weeks* in a *Lunar Quarter*.

The aggregate of *Pips*, or *Spots*, calculated in the following manner, amount to *three hundred and sixty-five*, or the number of *Days* in a *Year:*

The number in each Suite is	55
Multiply by four Suites	4
The number of Pips in the Pack	220

which he has in his hand is that which shall decide, or give a true answer to the Question which he had previously written out.

Reference having been now made to the Mystical Table, the corresponding Card to that which has been cut is to be found out thereon; and the Inquirer must then, by direction of the Priestess, write down on the same slip of paper, as before, the number which is attached thereto.

The Priestess is now, with due solemnity, to open the Book, and to turn to those pages which correspond with the Mystical Number belonging to the Card. Having referred to the Symbol, which corresponds with the Cœlestial Sign that presides over the subject in question, she is to read aloud the sacred passage which is placed opposite to it, and which will be found to be the true and unerring Answer to the Question asked.

For the sake of example, I shall suppose that the Inquirer had cut the Eight of Diamonds, which is numbered XXVII. in the Mystical Table; and that the Question asked was, "*Give me some information respecting the property which I have lost?*" On opening the Book at page XXVII., the following Answer will be found, under the Symbol of LEO, or the Celestial Lion, viz.: *Detection will take place whenever the stolen property is exposed for sale.*" Similarly appropriate Answers will be given to all other Questions which may be put.

THE FORTUNATE DAY.

In order to secure as favorable a result as the Fates will allow, it is certainly the most judicious plan to fix upon Fridays as the days most suitable for consultation. This day has been held mystical, and, as it were, set apart from the other days of the week, both in

---

Four Knaves, equivalent to, or counting eleven each	44
Four Queens, equivalent to twelve each	48
Four Kings, equivalent to thirteen each	52
Ace of Spades, as chief, counting	1
The number of Pips in the Pack, and of Days in a Year	365

OR,

The number of Pips in a Pack	220
Twelve Court Cards, multiplied by ten	120
The number of Court Cards	12
The number of Cards in each Suite	13
Total	365

OR,

The number of Pips on common Cards	220
Pips on Court Cards	12
Four Knaves, each counting ten more	40
Four Queens, each counting eleven more	44
Four Kings, each counting twelve more	48
Ace of Spades, as chief	1
Total	365

ancient and modern times; and assuredly, from my own experience, I can truly state that the ORACLE has, in nine cases out of ten, been propitious to those persons, of all nations, who have done me the honor to consult me *on a Friday*. It was for this reason that during all the other days of the week I steadily refused an interview with the Russian Autocrat, and the other illustrious strangers who were in France in 1815, as I feared that an *unfavorable* Answer might prejudice me in their opinion; seeing they might apprehend that I was predetermined to portend ill-luck and misfortune to men who, though victorious, were still looked on with hatred by many of my countrymen.

So well was my excellent and lamented patron, the Emperor Napoleon, aware of the fortunate day, that *twice only*, during the whole course of our acquaintance, did he consult me on any other day; and the Answers which he then received, with their almost immediate fulfilment, were such as justified him in abstaining, ever after, from consulting me, *except on a Friday*. I am tempted to relate here a curious circumstance which happened in 1809. Being in the neighborhood of St. Cloud on a Tuesday, I sent a servant with my humble duty to the Emperor, requesting an interview respecting a favor which I wished to be granted to one of my nephews. Napoleon returned me a note, saying "that he greatly desired an interview; but as there were matters of great moment which he had to consult me upon, he feared that he should be tempted to *put the Question* at once; and that he was therefore afraid to trust himself with me till Friday, when he should pay me a visit, and grant my petition." The Emperor came, accordingly, and I feel gratification when I look back, that the ORACLE, in this instance, was consulted with peculiar advantages both to the Sovereign and the Empire at large. I allude to the *victory of Wagram* and the *peace of Vienna*. I have adduced this instance, as the strongest in my recollection, of the propriety of adhering to a rule which I consider to be *indispensable* for propitiating the cœlestial bodies which rule over our destinies.

VICTORINE LE NORMAND.

TABLE OF THE CŒLESTIAL SIGNS,

WHICH INFLUENCE THE DESTINIES OF MEN.

ARIES—*THE RAM*, PRESIDES OVER Absent Friends and Relatives.	♈
TAURUS—*THE BULL*, PRESIDES OVER Travellers by Sea and Land.	♉
GEMINI—*THE TWINS*, PRESIDE OVER Friendship and Enmity.	♊
CANCER—*THE CRAB*, PRESIDES OVER Health and Longevity.	♋
LEO—*THE LION*, PRESIDES OVER Property Lost or Mislaid.	♌
VIRGO—*THE VIRGIN*, PRESIDES OVER Love and Courtship.	♍
LIBRA—*THE BALANCE*, PRESIDES OVER Promotion, Wealth, and Fortune.	♎
SCORPIO—*THE SCORPION*, PRESIDES OVER Males who desire Marriage.	♏
SAGITTARIUS—*THE ARCHER*, PRESIDES OVER Success in any Undertaking.	♐
CAPRICORNUS—*THE GOAT*, PRESIDES OVER Public and Private Events.	♑
AQUARIUS—*THE WATERMAN*, PRESIDES OVER Happiness and Misfortunes.	♒
PISCES—*THE FISHES*, PRESIDE OVER Females who desire Marriage.	♓

CORRESPONDING QUESTIONS,

WHICH ARE TO BE PUT TO THE ORACLE.

I wish to hear News of my relations and friends?

Is it necessary or proper that I should ever quit my native land?

What have I to expect from FRIENDS, or to fear from ENEMIES?

Shall I enjoy Health, and live long?

Give me some Information respecting the Property which I have lost?

Let me know some interesting Particulars relating to the Object of my Affections?

Inform me whether I shall ever be Promoted, Wealthy, or Fortunate?

Exhibit to me, M—— N—— (*here the Name of the Inquirer is to be inserted*), my Matrimonial Prospects?

What will be the result of my present undertaking?

I desire to obtain an Insight into those future Events, public or private, which affect my Interests.

Shall I enjoy Happiness, or suffer Misfortunes, in this life?

Exhibit to me, E—— C—— (*here the Name of the Inquirer is to be inserted*), my Matrimonial Prospects?

I.

♈	They are in expectation of great riches.
♉	Thou shalt soon have to perform a journey.
♊	Thou hast no real enemy.
♋	Thou shalt live long.
♌	Seek diligently, and the lost will be found.
♍	Thy love will be returned without measure.
♎	Thy fortunes shall flourish.
♏	Thou shalt wed a shrew; but be courageous under adverse fortune; her perverse disposition will shorten her life.
♐	Your utmost hopes will be realized.
♑	A rich harvest may be expected.
♒	There is no rose without a thorn.
♓	Marriage will increase thy wealth, and prolong thy life.

II.

They are in good health.	♈
Thy safety depends on staying at home.	♉
A secret enemy is now circumventing thee. Take heed, lest thou fall!	♊
You will enjoy tolerable health, and live to see your utmost wishes realized.	♋
There is every probability that it will soon be found.	♌
Marriage will take place between you, before many weeks are past.	♍
For a time, thou shalt not be very fortunate;—but persevere.	♎
Matrimony will not improve your fortunes.	♏
Be not too sanguine, lest a failure take place.	♐
Two powerful kingdoms are about to be engaged in war.	♑
You will enjoy more happiness in old age, than in your youth.	♒
Little wealth; but a numerous progeny.	♓

III.

♈	They labor under heavy difficulties.
♉	A period will soon arrive, when it will be necessary for thee to remove to a far country.
♊	Thy friends will greatly assist in promoting thy welfare.
♋	Your days will be lengthened by sobriety and early rising.
♌	You have lost little, in comparison with what you soon shall gain.
♍	You may hope, in due time, to obtain the object of your choice.
♎	Thou shalt die, possessed of great riches.
♏	A handsome and good-natured wife
♐	You may rest satisfied that the result will be favorable.
♑	Dreadful events are about to occur; but they need not disturb thee.
♒	You will enjoy a moderate share of happiness, throughout your whole life.
♓	Matrimony is not calculated to render you happy.

IV.

One of them is preparing for a long journey.	♈
Thou shalt have to sail over the salt sea, for many a league.	♉
Much harm is intended thee; but thou mayest avoid it by care and circumspection.	♊
Your health will not be affected by change of climate.	♋
Be circumspect, and you will soon recover that which is missing.	♌
Let the choice of thy partner be founded on prudence: set not thy mind on beauty!	♍
Promotion awaits thee.	♎
An imprudent alliance.	♏
Success will attend your exertions.	♐
A short war will be succeeded by peace of long duration.	♑
Thou shalt enjoy much domestic comfort and happiness.	♒
A large family and an empty larder.	♓

V.

♈	They are greatly troubled at not hearing from thee.
♉	A long journey is before thee.
♊	Beware of flattery from a pretended friend!
♋	Your children's children will sport around you.
♌	By seeking after that which hath been lost, you will sacrifice much time and patience, without benefit.
♍	The object of thy affections will soon communicate with thee, by *letter*.
♎	Thou art more fortunate than thousands of thy companions.
♏	Poverty in the outset; but a fortune rapidly amassed by industry:—many children!
♐	Make up your mind to meet with disappointments.
♑	Violent and lasting war in the *East*.
♒	You will experience alternate changes of happiness and misfortune.
♓	You will be blessed with an affectionate husband:—Do all in your power to merit his kindness.

VI.

One of them does not mean thee fair.	♈
Thy fortune will be greatly increased by emigration.	♉
Be cautious in the selection of thy friends: particularly among those who make large professions.	♊
You will count eighty-three summers!	♋
It will be found, but not for some time.	♌
Your suit will meet with encouragement.	♍
Better be born lucky than rich!	♎
A wife, whose acquirements will produce much wealth.	♏
You were born under an unlucky planet!	♐
A great rise in the public securities may be expected.	♑
If riches confer happiness, you shall possess an ample share.	♒
Reject a *jealous* lover: he will never permit you to enjoy peace, or the least happiness.	♓

VII.

♈	Thou shalt soon be visited by some of them.
♉	In a neighboring country thou shalt meet with one who will captivate thy affections.
♊	Your fortune will be promoted by the active and disinterested exertions of your friends.
♋	You will be afflicted with gout.
♌	It has been unfairly taken away from thee; but the thief will be discovered.
♍	You will have to contend with a wealthy rival.
♎	Great fortune will be thy lot.
♏	A handsome wife: but one who will give you no little cause for jealousy.
♐	If you are careful, you will undoubtedly prosper in this affair.
♑	A public event will take place, from which thou mayest expect great benefit.
♒	Difficulties will surround you; but do not despond, for in the end is much happiness.
♓	The man whom you are destined to marry is at present in a foreign land.

VIII.

One, in particular, wishes to see thee.	♈
Thou shalt soon receive an advantageous offer for emigration.	♉
An enemy, who intended thee much ill, has failed in his machinations and greatly injured himself.	♊
You will live long, and die much regretted.	♋
You will recover it in a most surprising and unexpected manner.	♌
Thy partner in life shall be very wealthy.	♍
Thou shalt be wealthy, but not contented.	♎
A morose, ill-tempered spouse, with a small portion of wealth.	♏
There is nothing which can prevent the completion of your wishes.	♐
A man of high station will soon arrive in this country, to whom thou mayest look for preferment.	♑
You will meet with vicissitudes; but strength of mind will support you under every trial.	♒
Your husband will be inclined to jealousy and ill-humor:—see that you give him no cause for either.	♓

IX.

♈	They have just received disagreeable intelligence.
♉	A great fortune awaits thy acceptance, in the East.
♊	An avowed enemy will soon become thy sincere friend.
♋	A malignant fever will seize you:—despair not;—you will recover, and live many years!
♌	It is gone from thee for ever!—Give thyself no further trouble.
♍	Beware lest disparity of temper lead to unhappiness for life.
♎	Fortune will crown thy exertions.
♏	A frugal and industrious spouse, who will contribute greatly to your health and wealth!
♐	A designing female will prevent a happy termination of this affair.
♑	A domestic calamity will afflict thee for a short season.
♒	In youth, Care!—In age, Competence and Content!
♓	Your present affections will be disappointed; but in the end you will have cause for gladness.—You will meet with a more agreeable companion.

X.

One of them has succeeded to great fortune.	♈
Prosperity will attend thee, only by remaining at home.	♉
One whom you think a staunch friend will soon prove himself unworthy of the name.	♊
Your health will remain good for many years; but your desire for longevity is in vain.	♋
Search well:—in the most remote corner you may chance to find it.	♌
Your lover is fickle; but with due encouragement may still remain constant.	♍
Be not over-anxious after riches;—they will not bring thee happiness.	♎
An helpmate who will call you *cuckold!*	♏
If you be not discouraged, you may easily attain the object of your wishes.	♐
Beware of meddling in public matters;—they would affect thee greatly in thy fortunes.	♑
It is thy fate to taste more of the bitter, than of the sweets, of life.	♒
The stars have long since indicated, that you shall marry a wealthy merchant.	♓

XI.

♈	A marriage has taken place among thy relatives.
♉	Advancement awaits thee in a foreign land.
♊	You have little to expect from the one, or to fear from the other.
♋	Long life is promised to you, if you quit not your native country.
♌	Thy utmost efforts will prove ineffectual;—the Oracle can only caution thee to be more circumspect in future.
♍	Success in your suit will excite much envy, in a certain quarter.
♎	Thou shalt have a fortune bequeathed to thee.
♏	A wife of a fair complexion, with blue eyes, and a placid temper.
♐	Your patience will be greatly tried; but final success may be looked for.
♑	A crowned head will soon be laid low.
♒	The path is rugged over which you are to tread.
♓	You will have a splendid offer of marriage, from a native of a foreign land, who will require you to quit your own country

XII.

One of thy relatives is on the road to see thee.	♈
Tarry in the land of thy nativity; for there only shalt thou find happiness!	♉
Be not too sanguine:—all are not friends who are honored by that name!	♊
You will enjoy health, and live to comb gray hairs.	♋
A female shall find it for thee.	♌
Wed not in haste; if you do, you may repent at leisure.	♍
Fortune will be thine by marriage.	♎
An ill-favored spouse, but one whose tongue will give you greater cause of lamentation than her want of beauty.	♏
Fortune favors the brave!—Let no accident discourage you.	♐
Rebellion in the South:—the consequences for a time will be dreadful!	♑
Many years of unalloyed bliss are in store for you.	♒
You are destined to die an old maid.	♓

XIII.

♈	Beware of treachery among thy supposed friends!
♉	Be industrious at home, and there will be no necessity for seeking riches abroad.
♊	There is one who will use great exertion to undermine thee in thy affections.
♋	Avoid dissipation, and your life will be greatly prolonged.
♌	Make timely application to the Civil authority.
♍	Your marriage will not take place for some time:—Be patient, and you will behold wonders!
♎	However impoverished thou mayest be, thy children shall be wealthy.
♏	Beauty, wit, and fortune will constitute the dowry of thy beloved spouse!
♐	Put your trust in Providence, and He will not desert you in time of need.
♑	News of a great battle will soon arrive.
♒	By endeavoring to render others happy, you, yourself, will be completely so.
♓	You will be more nice than wise in the choice of a husband.

XIV.

The sun of good fortune now shines upon thy family.	♈
In a city two hundred leagues from hence, thy genius will procure thee much gain.	♉
Beware of telling thy warmest friend more of thy affairs than is barely requisite.	♊
You shall!—So the Planet, under which you were born, decrees.	♋
You will have little cause to regret what hath been lost.	♌
You will not find happiness, unless all friends are made acquainted with your intended union.	♍
Thou shalt have more wealth than brains.	♎
The hair of thy destined spouse will resemble the sand on the shores of the Red Sea whilst her temper will be as unstable and raging as its waters, in a storm.	♏
A sea-faring man will step between you and the completion of your desires.	♐
The commerce of this country will soon be greatly extended beyond its present limits.	♑
The partner of your bed will long render you supremely happy.	♒
The Planets decree that you are not to marry the man you love!	♓

XV.

♈	An increase has just taken place in the family of one of thy friends.
♉	An opportunity will soon present itself of advancing thy fortunes at home.
♊	Thou shalt assuredly meet with many friends. See that thou preserve them as such.
♋	Your health will remain vigorous to a good old age.
♌	Be silent and cautious and a wonderful discovery will be made.
♍	You will meet with opposition from the parents or relatives of the person whom you love.
♎	Seek not after wealth;—it will be thy bane!
♏	A beloved wife, who will bear to you fifteen children; the majority of whom will be the comfort of your life, and the staff of your age.
♐	A lucky Planet presides over thy destinies, and will guide thee in thy course.
♑	The independence of a small but flourishing republic in the West will speedily be acknowledged.
♒	The irritability of your own temper will be a great barrier to your happiness.
♓	Decline every offer of marriage for six months; you will thus be free to make a most advantageous choice.

XVI.

They enjoy health, and desire to see thee.	♈
Thy journeyings will be prosperous!	♉
Thou hast a bitter enemy; but return good for evil.	♊
Commit no excess, and thy days will be lengthened.	♋
It is mislaid.	♌
Pursue not the object of your affections too ardently.	♍
Wealth awaits thee;—use it well.	♎
Thou shalt assuredly wed one who will prove both a vixen and a slut;—but droop not if thou art unfortunate, for a second marriage will compensate thy sufferings.	♏
Thou shalt be successful.	♐
The aspect of the Planets portends war!	♑
Look not for much happiness on earth.	♒
A speedy and advantageous marriage; but no progeny!	♓

XVII.

♈	Those thou inquirest after wish thee among them
♉	Travel not far!
♊	Thine enemies are powerful.
♋	Health, but not longevity.
♌	Renew thy search.
♍	Thy love will in due time be returned.
♎	Be not too anxious after worldly affairs.
♏	It is likely that thou shalt meet with a sad disaster in the marriage state:—watch thy spouse well!
♐	Courage insures success.
♑	Peace at home: but war abroad.
♒	No sinister event shall mar thy happiness.
♓	Matrimony without much love.

XVIII.

Misfortunes press heavily upon them at present.	♈
If thou quittest thy country, dangers will beset thee both by sea and land.	♉
Nothing!	♊
Some of your relatives will wish you dead, that they may inherit your riches; but you will outlive many of them.	♋
Be slow in suspecting:—it will be found in due season.	♌
Your lover will prove true as the needle to the pole!	♍
Thirst not after riches; they would but prove thy destruction!	♎
Thy helpmate will persecute thee with her tongue; but let not trifles daunt thee.	♏
Proceed cautiously, and prosper!	♐
An important circumstance will occur in thy family!	♑
There is no happiness without alloy.	♒
A rich and kind husband, with a numerous race of descendants.	♓

XIX.

♈	They are about to dispatch a rich present for thee.
♉	Thou art destined to travel far.
♊	A secret enemy is lurking near thee:—Beware of him!!
♋	Though in youth you enjoy but poor health, your old age will be strong and vigorous.
♌	The recovery is so uncertain, that, if found, it would hardly recompense thy labor and expense.
♍	You have cause to fear a successful rival!
♎	It will be thine own fault if thou art not rich.
♏	Thou shalt be united to a rich widow, whose love for thee will be extreme; but whose jealousy will cause thee much uneasiness.
♐	A relative will cause disappointment to thy hopes.
♑	Insurrection in the North; but it will have a speedy and a happy termination.
♒	During a few years of your life you will feel the heavy hand of misfortune!
♓	Thy husband will spend much time and money at the gaming-table; but thou mayest reclaim him.

XX.

A female relative is about to be led to the altar.	♈
Honors and wealth await thee in a foreign nation.	♉
A friend whom you little dream of will greatly improve your fortune.	♊
Residence in the country, with temperance, will prolong your life for many years.	♋
It will be found ere the sun rises and sets three times.	♌
If you be not careful, the person whom you love will soon be engaged to another.	♍
A lucky speculation will enrich thee.	♎
The Planets portend a happy marriage with the object of thy affections.	♏
The cup will be dashed from thy lips just as thou art about to taste its sweets.	♐
A brave nation will soon recover its ancient rights, territories, and glorious name.	♑
Your happiness or misery will depend on your own conduct, except in one particular instance.	♒
He whom you love will wed another; but your happiness will be secured by a more propitious alliance!	♓

XXI.

♈	One of them is confined to a sick chamber.
♉	You will soon have to perform a long journey.
♊	Much!
♋	Thy partner will involve thee in troubles which will greatly impair thy health.
♌	The offer of a small reward will lead to speedy recovery.
♍	Should you lose your present favorite, you will have no cause to be sad.
♎	If thou goest abroad, thou shalt return heavily laden with gold and silver.
♏	A beautiful virgin will grace thy bridal bed.
♐	A secret enemy is undermining thy interests in this affair.
♑	A long established and once powerful empire is tottering to its fall.
♒	You will never have much cause to be elated with joy, nor to be oppressed by sorrow.
♓	A short courtship, a hasty marriage, and plenty of time for repentance!

XXII.

A letter is about to be addressed to thee, containing glad tidings of them	♈
Nothing should induce thee to stir from home.	♉
Thy best friend is at present exerting himself for thy welfare.	♊
The Star which presided over your birth will continue to do so until your ninety-third year.	♋
The thief will only for a short period escape detection.	♌
Guard your heart against the shafts of love for some time; when you will meet with an object worthy of your choice.	♍
Trade will procure thee wealth.	♎
Four wives are allotted to thee, viz.:—one who shall be slothful—a true virgin—an industrious helpmate—and a widow of advanced age.	♏
The celestial bodies which influence the destinies of men are favorable to thy wishes.	♐
A great diminution of taxes is in contemplation.	♑
Your happiness will be centered in an excellent partner, and a numerous offspring.	♒
Thy marriage will excite envy among thy female acquaintances; but felicity is thy lot!	♓

XXIII.

♈	They are in full expectation that thou wilt visit them soon.
♉	It is necessary; and will prove beneficial to thee and thine.
♊	Depend on thyself only; for friends are fickle!—Foes thou needst not fear!
♋	You will number sixty years of health and happiness!
♌	It will be recovered through the instrumentality of a child.
♍	Let not wealth alone induce you to marry:—it will not suffice to make you happy without mutual affection.
♎	Honorable conduct will be the cause of thy promotion.
♏	The Stars forbid thee to enter into the state of wedlock!
♐	Many endeavors will be made to prevent thy success; but they will fail.
♑	A most important law will soon be passed, which will greatly affect thee.
♒	A happy medium is thy portion.
♓	You will marry a man more than double your own age:—he will, nevertheless, make you a happy wife.

XXIV.

Thy last letter to them hath miscarried; and they grieve that they are forgotten by thee.	♈
In a foreign land much wealth awaits thee.	♉
A true friend will bequeath to you a great fortune	♊
Health and longevity will be thy portion, if thou avoidest the mixtures of the pharmacopolist.	♋
Accident will lead to a discovery.	♌
You will meet with a disappointment in love.	♍
A rich relative will bequeath thee much wealth.	♎
Thou shalt find more happiness in the married than in a single life.	♏
Thou shalt succeed beyond thy utmost hopes.	♐
An event will shortly occur in which the ruin of many is involved. Be thou wary!	♑
Thou art destined to be healthy and wealthy:—be virtuous likewise, and happiness will follow.	♒
You will marry a man who is young, handsome, and wealthy:—you will be greatly beloved by him.	♓

XXV.

♈	A large fortune is bequeathed among thy family:—see that thou hast thy share.
♉	Most assuredly it would be improper!
♊	The malice of your enemies will avail but little, if your own actions can bear scrutiny.
♋	Health! but a small share of happiness in this world.
♌	All will be revealed unto thee in a dream:—see thou attend to the suggestions of the vision!
♍	True love never did run smooth;—how can you expect it to be otherwise in your case.
♎	Persevere and thou shalt be fortunate.
♏	A scold is destined to be thy bride. Due chastisement produceth reformation.
♐	Thou shalt be unsuccessful!
♑	There will soon be a great fall in the prices of all the necessaries of life.
♒	The Stars portend that a circumstance is about to happen which will decide your future happiness or misery.
♓	You are destined to be the third wife of a wealthy man.

XXVI.

Thou mayest expect disagreeable news respecting them.	♈
If thou art wise, tarry at home!	♉
Thou hast many friends who would, but cannot, assist thee. Thy future fortune depends solely on thyself.	♊
Anxiety and exertion in the accumulation of riches will impair thy health, and shorten life.	♋
That which thou supposedst lost has only been too carefully laid aside.	♌
Your career of courtship will be short; but marriage and lasting happiness will spring from it.	♍
Prosperity will be the reward of thy industry.	♎
If you marry for three years to come, misfortunes will befall you. Be patient!	♏
News from abroad will greatly alter the face of thy affairs, as well as thy views respecting this adventure.	♐
A new religion is about to be established, to which there will be innumerable converts.	♑
A grievous misfortune will overtake you; but keep a stout heart, for peace of mind will follow.	♒
Your husband's unkindness will render you unhappy; but the affectionate regards of your children will be a source of great joy.	♓

XXVII.

♈	One of them intends to leave thee a sum of money at his death:—see that thy conduct do not frustrate his intentions.
♉	You will meet with better fortune abroad than you would at home.
♊	Though friends are scarce, consider thyself fortunate in having no enemies.
♋	Thy wish for health shall be gratified; but desire not old age and infirmities.
♌	Detection will take place whenever the stolen property is exposed for sale.
♍	Let not infatuation lead thee, at present, to fix thy affections unalterably.
♎	The first deviation from the paths of rectitude will be the commencement of misfortune to thee.
♏	Thy spouse will be no helpmate to thee!
♐	Thy mind may rest satisfied in the expectation of a happy result.
♑	An important communication is about to take place between this country and the most powerful nation of the East.
♒	The celestial bodies which presided at thy birth were to thee the harbingers of good fortune!
♓	Your husband's fondness for the bottle will lessen his attachment to you, unless by kindness and constant attention you wean him from it.

XXVIII.

One of thy relatives is about to be greatly exalted.	♈
At the time of thy nativity, thou wert destined to flourish in a strange land.	♉
You will suffer materially from the machinations of a false friend.	♊
A placid temper will insure to you health and long life.	♋
Spend no more time in searching after that which no perseverance can recover.	♌
The object of thy affections will soon have to perform a long journey. This will not prevent your marriage.	♍
Thou shalt find a rich treasure.	♎
Thy spouse will bring thee a fortune, which will be the cause of much quarreling betwixt you.	♏
Partial success:—but be not discouraged; for thy next undertaking, of the same nature, will be more prosperous.	♐
The government of a neighboring nation is about to be thrown into great embarrassment.	♑
Your hopes of happiness will be fulfilled, through the kind attentions of your friends.	♒
You will act wisely in declining a clandestine marriage, which will be proposed to you. Better prospects are in store for you!	♓

XXIX.

♈	Thy friends look daily for thy appearance amongst them.
♉	Thou shalt go abroad:—dangers will surround thee, but thou shalt return wealthy and happy!
♊	Thy friends are inclined to do thee much good:—let nothing on thy part induce them to swerve from their intentions.
♋	Desire not so much length of days as health to enjoy them;—which will be thy lot.
♌	Thine eyes shall never again behold it. Be more careful in future!
♍	You will not see your beloved for some time.
♎	Thy fortune depends on thy integrity.
♏	Your bride will be young, beautiful, and accomplished. Watch over her health.
♐	Ultimate success!
♑	Great events are about to take place, which will excite astonishment throughout the whole civilized world.
♒	The death of a relative will cause you great grief.
♓	Thou shalt wed a man six feet in height:—his manners and conduct will be extremely pleasing and praiseworthy.

XXX.

They are full of gayety, but a cloud will soon overshadow them.	♈
Thou hast nothing to fear, but much to expect, from going abroad.	♉
Fear nothing!—thy greatest enemy is rendered powerless.	♊
Be virtuous, and you will be happy; be temperate, and you will enjoy health; rise early, and you will live long.	♋
Thou suspectest wrongfully; turn thine eyes in another direction.	♌
Thou art fated to behold another, who will inspire thee with stronger affection than thy present favorite.	♍
Bear up against the frowns of the world, and, in the end, thou shalt be rich.	♎
A beautiful and virtuous wife! She will be the mother of a numerous progeny, who will inherit her perfections.	♏
Failure without remedy, if you persevere.	♐
A violent political storm is about to burst forth.	♑
You will speedily be enriched; and, if you abuse not your wealth, a happy life is before you.	♒
A rustic is destined to be thy husband; his wealth and goodness of heart will compensate for his want of polish.	♓

XXXI.

♈	Their worldly concerns prosper greatly; but a reverse is to be apprehended.
♉	Thou shalt soon be transported to a far country!
♊	Thou hast a powerful enemy;—beware of him!
♋	You are safe from all accidents by sea and land which may affect your health. Let not vice bring on disease.
♌	Be patient!—the thief will become conscience-struck and confess all.
♍	Your love is too romantic, and will yield but short happiness. Think deeply before you wed!
♎	Matrimony will elevate thee above all want.
♏	Thou shalt marry a woman twice thine own age;—she will bring thee store of wealth.
♐	Permanent advantage!
♑	A long series of very fine weather may be expected.
♒	Your relatives will cause you much trouble.
♓	Beware of the artifices of a villain who would deceive thee with false pretenses:—your next lover will be worthy of you.

XXXII.

One of them has just been blessed with a male heir.	♈
In a distant land thou shalt meet with one who will be thy partner for the remainder of thy days.	♉
A female friend will serve thee in time of need and peril.	♊
A life of much enjoyment; but not warranted to last long!	♋
A female is in fault;—be merciful!	♌
Your sincerity is doubted by the object of your affections. A speedy explanation will do you service.	♍
Look out for a rich partner in life:—thou mayest find one, be assured.	♎
Thy wife, though rich and beautiful, will cause thee much sorrow by her pride and haughty demeanor.	♏
Your expectations of success are liable to be marred by procrastination and delay.	♐
The career of a hero has commenced, whose talents will eclipse those of all others who have gone before him.	♑
Pecuniary losses will occasion to you great uneasiness.	♒
Thy husband will be a soldier of rank:—see that thou remain faithful to him whilst he is fighting the battles of his country.	♓

XXXIII.

♈	Surprising news concerning one of them will soon reach thee.
♉	Some important event will soon occur which will prevent all idea of going abroad.
♊	Thy friends esteem, and will serve thee on the first opportunity.
♋	A timely application to the physician will prolong your life.
♌	It will be found ere many days are past.
♍	Continue thy attachment, but avoid a hasty marriage:—it would impair thy fortunes!
♎	Prosperity in the autumn of your days!
♏	The tongue of thy spouse will resemble a two-edged sword—cutting both ways—by day and by night. Argument will not prevail; blows only can blunt it.
♐	Thy exertions, if continued with spirit, will shortly be crowned with success.
♑	A grand discovery, important to all Europe, is about to take place.
♒	You will be more fortunate than wise.
♓	Marriage, wealth, and retirement, will secure thy happiness from any interruption.

XXXIV.

Thou shalt soon behold one of thy dearest friends.	♈
By journeying northward thy wealth will be greatly increased.	♉
A powerful friend will counteract the malice of thy foes.	♊
An accident will occur before your fiftieth year, which will greatly impair your health.	♋
The police only can sift this matter to the bottom; but the business will be attended with much trouble.	♌
The object of your attachment has many virtues, but likewise some faults, which will be made known to thee anon.	♍
No misfortunes will assail thee; but thou canst never be wealthy.	♎
A sad prospect, if thou art too precipitate!—poverty and misery in all its shapes and forms!	♏
A happy termination depends on co-operation with the person whom you love most.	♐
Revolution in the West;—the result of which will long be doubtful.	♑
Marriage and retirement will give you much happiness.	♒
Thou shalt marry a man high in favor with his sovereign.	♓

XXXV.

♈	They have much cause to regret thy absence from them at this time.
♉	Thou shalt never quit thy native country.
♊	By the artful suggestions of an enemy to thy peace, thou art liable to fall into peril.
♋	Dissipation shortens life:—Beware! Live temperately!
♌	Examine strictly the countenance of the second person thou seest to-morrow morning.
♍	There is no cause why thy love should be disturbed by jealous apprehensions. Thou art truly beloved!
♎	Fortune will favor thee;—be assured, and doubt not.
♏	If the relatives on both sides are not favorable to the connection which you expect to form, you will have but little share of happiness.
♐	A decided failure, if you proceed.
♑	Violent storms are portended! No injury will result to thee or thine.
♒	A lucky enterprise will give you great cause of contentment.
♓	A serious misunderstanding between thyself and thy husband will occasion thee much grief.

XXXVI.

One of thy female friends has just brought forth a daughter.	♈
By upright dealing thou mayest attain great wealth in a distant island.	♉
Your enemies will triumph for a short season; but your ultimate success will put them to shame.	♊
In a warmer climate your health will remain uninjured; and your days will be lengthened.	♋
A dog will be the discoverer!	♌
Give not thy heart up to the sweet enticements of love, but be patient for a season, when thou shalt behold one who will glad thy heart!	♍
A large sum of money will be bequeathed to thee, by one from whom thou hadst no hopes.	♎
In a foreign land thou shalt find one who will render thy life comfortable and happy.	♏
If you knew all, you would at once perceive that the undertaking will prove fruitless.	♐
An expedition, lately gone from this country, will soon return crowned with success.	♑
You will, at no distant period, hear news of a disagreeable nature.	♒
A nobleman is destined to be thy bridegroom. Let thy conduct be worthy of thy exalted rank.	♓

XXXVII.

♈	A large party of thy friends are now indulging in mirth and jollity. They grasp the wine-cup, and drink to thy prosperity.
♉	The Stars declare that illness, perhaps death, would be thy fate in a foreign land.
♊	Gentleness of disposition, on thy part, will secure thee many friends!—one will prove himself a friend indeed!
♋	You will arrive at a good old age; but your temper will become so irritable as to annoy all around you.
♌	Let no persuasion induce thee to continue a search after that which is irrevocably gone from thee.
♍	Marriage between you and your beloved is ardently desired by those who have an influence over your fortunes.
♎	A female relative will leave thee a handsome estate.
♏	Thou shalt wed the second daughter of a rich man, whose name begins with D. The name of thy bride begins with E.
♐	To unwearied exertion nothing is impossible. Persevere!
♑	A great change is about to take place among statesmen of high rank.
♒	By marriage, a fortune will be yours which ought to make you happy.
♓	Thy time for marriage is not yet arrived:—by waiting patiently thy lot will be greatly bettered.

XXXVIII

One of them will soon have to visit a far province.	♈
Advancement awaits thee in a western province	♉
Thou art happy in the love of thy friends, and in their intentions to serve thee.	♊
To live long, there are three things which you must avoid, viz.:—High buildings, voyages by sea, and the sparkling goblet!	♋
In less than three weeks it shall be found.	♌
Suffer not thy soul to be enslaved by the enchanting delusions of love, whilst affairs of greater moment claim thy attention.	♍
Thy promotion will be rapid and satisfactory.	♎
The hair of thy bride will be like the wing of the raven; her eye like the sparkling diamond; her teeth like pearls sunk in a bed of coral; and her cheek like the opening rose!	♏
Under the present aspect of the heavenly bodies, a successful termination appears improbable, but not impossible.	♐
A most infamous political intrigue is now carrying on:—it will be discovered.	♑
You will be particularly fortunate in business.	♒
Thou hast not yet seen the man to whom thou art to be irrevocably united:—on the hundredth day from the present thou shalt behold him!	♓

XXXIX.

♈	A proposition is about to be made to thee by them which it will be prudent for thee to accede to.
♉	The Stars portend great success to thy exertions in a distant colony.
♊	A foe will injure thee; but the laws of thy country will afford thee ample redress.
♋	As health is the reward of temperance, so premature old age is brought on by excess. Take heed!
♌	Let no persuasion induce thee to give up a diligent search after thy goods.
♍	Thy beloved is at present occupied by thoughts which pertain to thy happiness;—a meeting between you will soon take place.
♎	Be frugal, industrious, and honorable in thy dealings; and riches will pour in upon thee!
♏	If thou shouldst wed the dame on whom thou hast set thy affections, thou shalt find a hidden treasure!
♐	Pecuniary aid is required to insure success.
♑	An important change is about to take place in thy family!
♒	Industry and frugality in your youth will render your old age happy and respected.
♓	Enter not into the bands of wedlock with thy present admirer:—it would be productive of much loss and pain unto thee.

XL.

The birth of a son causes much gladness in the family of one of thy friends.	♈
You will acquire wealth at home;—use it wisely!	♉
A sincere friend will relieve thee from an embarrassment into which one of thy foes will plunge thee.	♊
Your constitution will remain strong until the forty-first year.	♋
Give up all suspicion of dishonesty, and commence a minute search.	♌
Beware of the allurements of wantonness; and let not corrupt desires defile the pure and gentle stream of true affection.	♍
Trouble not thyself respecting wealth;—it would only make thee unhappy.	♎
A blue-eyed daughter of the North will consent to be thy bride:—search her out; she hath wealth in abundance.	♏
The advantage to be derived will not compensate the labor and expense attending your pursuit.	♐
Peace is about to take place between two contending powers:—it will not be lasting.	♑
Thou shalt possess wealth, but it will not make thee happy.	♒
You will have two offers of marriage about the same time. Reject him who has most wealth. Accept him whose disposition is most congenial to your own.	♓

XLI.

♈	Their affairs are in that state, that it is necessary thou shouldst soon visit them.
♉	No!
♊	Be cautious that he, who says he is thy sincere friend, may not prove thy bitter foe.
♋	At the age of seventy-nine years your teeth will be renewed.
♌	Be not discouraged in thy search. Success attends perseverance!
♍	Let nothing divert thy affections from their present object:—thy love will in due time be rewarded, and happiness will attend you both!
♎	Seek not after riches, but be contented with thy lot!
♏	Thou shalt visit the Eastern Indies, where it will be the fate of a female, who possesses great riches, to call thee husband.
♐	Pecuniary embarrassments will prevent the successful completion of your desires.
♑	Great losses by sea!
♒	You will find happiness in a foreign land.
♓	Thy husband will tyrannize over thee:—thy children will love and comfort thee.

XLII.

One of them is using much interest in procuring patronage for thee.	♈
In a distant clime thou shalt meet with one who will contribute greatly to the raising of thy fortune.	♉
On the first opportunity the former will endeavor to injure you; the latter are about to load you with benefits.	♊
Equanimity and temperance, only, will insure you health and long life.	♋
An inmate of thy house will recover the lost property.	♌
Let thy affection be genuine and pure; so will it be appreciated by thy beloved;—for the madness of desire shall defeat its own pursuits.	♍
No extent of wealth would ever be a compensation to thee for the loss of thy peace of mind.	♎
A virtuous wife will bear to thee many children; whilst thine own industry will greatly increase thy wealth.	♏
Give up this pursuit; for, however fair the appearances, be assured it is hopeless.	♐
A comet, of immense size, will soon appear in the firmament.	♑
Your partner will be the cause of great sorrow to you.	♒
Strive not for the mastery over thy husband; for it will be his determination to keep thee under him.	♓

XLIII.

♈	They are about to send thee a sum of money.
♉	You will visit foreign countries, and thereby be enriched. Your latter days will be passed in tranquillity at home.
♊	A friend, whom you reckon little upon, will be the means of advancing you to great honors and fortune.
♋	Thy old age will be blessed by the affectionate regards and kind attentions of a numerous family.
♌	Examine minutely the buildings detached from thy house.
♍	Be no longer a suitor for the hand of one who is already affianced to another. Thou shalt soon perceive the truth!
♎	Thou wert born under a lucky Planet.
♏	You will wed more wealthily than happily!
♐	The Fates portend good luck!
♑	A silver mine will soon be discovered, of the profits of which thou shalt partake.
♒	Love will be to you the source of much happiness.
♓	The stature of thy bridegroom will approach to that of the dwarf;—use him gently, as thy happiness will depend on the length of his days.

XLIV.

Thou shalt soon receive agreeable news from one of them.	♈
Misfortunes will attend every step that you take out of your own country.	♉
You have a friend who will remain faithful to you under every change of circumstances.	♊
Traveling will improve your health; it will also lay the foundation of a strong constitution.	♋
A tall man could give thee sure information if he would. Try him!	♌
Open thine eyes and thou shalt behold a more desirable object than thy present favorite.	♍
Thy fortune will be moderate, but sufficient for all thy wants.	♎
A tender passion pervades the breast of an amiable woman, who will one day be thy wife.	♏
Just as you are about to grasp the fruits of this enterprise, you will be defeated by the malice of an enemy.	♐
Very general illness will shortly prevail!	♑
A clandestine marriage will produce great grief in your family.	♒
It is your fate to be left a widow with five children. A second husband will act the part of a kind parent unto them.	♓

XLV.

♈	One of them is about to be greatly trusted by men in power and authority.
♉	Absence from your native country, for a short season, will amend your fortune.
♊	One whom you reckon a friend will prove treacherous to your interests.
♋	Ill health will overtake you; but by due care your days will be prolonged.
♌	Thou mayest recover it by stratagem.
♍	Pursue steadily thy present attachment;—thy constancy will in due time meet with its reward.
♎	Thou shalt have a prize in the lottery!
♏	No circumstance ought to induce thee to marry for three years;—at the end of which period thou shalt behold one worthy of thy most ardent love.
♐	Pursue not this phantom any longer; for every prospect of success has vanished.
♑	The discovery of an extensive plot is at hand!
♒	It is your lot to meet with many difficulties:—still despair not, for you will surmount them all.
♓	You will be the wife of four husbands; all of whom you will survive:—so the Stars decree!

XLVI.

One of them is just recovering from a fit of severe illness.	♈
You will acquire a large fortune abroad, which you will have the pleasure of spending at home.	♉
The Planets declare that thine enemies will be caught in the nets which they spread for thee.	♊
Three-score and twelve years will be the limit of your mortal existence!	♋
Some sign will be shown thee to-day, whereby the property may be found.	♌
The affection of thy beloved is stronger even than thine.	♍
Riches would be to thee only the source of unbounded misery.	♎
Thou shalt wed an heiress! Cherish her!	♏
Success!	♐
Great scarcity will shortly prevail.	♑
A cottage and content are allotted to thee and thy helpmate.	♒
You will wed the handsomest man in the district to which you belong.	♓

XLVII.

♈	A great fraud has been committed on them. Thy care may rectify it.
♉	Yes;—for, thereby, thou shalt have much gain.
♊	Your friends will vary as your fortunes change.
♋	You will wed your third partner on the day you commence your seventy-sixth year!
♌	During thy search, a greater treasure will be found, than that which hath been lost.
♍	If thou lovest truly, thy suit will be successful.
♎	When thou art wealthy, which thou soon shalt be, see that thou forget not thy poor relations.
♏	Thou shalt wed an orphan; who, if she bring thee no dowry, will still prove a virtuous wife!
♐	Great disappointment!
♑	Active preparations for warfare are taking place in a neighboring country.
♒	After an active life passed in the busy world, you will enjoy the sweets of retirement.
♓	You will three times grace the bridal bed, and be the happy mother of nineteen children!

XLVIII.

They are about to be involved in litigation.	♈
Forsake not thy friends, relatives, and (beneficial though hidden) prospects at home, for uncertain fortune abroad.	♉
The malice of your foes will not affect you; whilst the good offices of your friends will confer permanent advantage.	♊
A sedentary life will cut off ten years from the natural period of your existence.	♋
Whilst thou art lamenting its loss, thy property might be found. Institute further inquiry!	♌
A person of envious disposition will endeavor to mar thy happiness, by speaking ill of thee to thy beloved. Be cautious!	♍
Thy desire for wealth shall be amply gratified.	♎
Beauty, Health, Wealth, and Happiness!—but of short duration!	♏
A kind female will secure to you every advantage you can desire.	♐
A new manufacture will be established, from which you and others will derive much advantage.	♑
Your offspring will cause you much trouble of mind; but in the end cometh happiness!	♒
A gray head will repose with thine, upon the same pillow. Cherish old age!	♓

XLIX.

♈	A serious misunderstanding and quarrel have taken place among them.
♉	If you quit your native country, your return is more than doubtful!
♊	Your greatest enemy will soon be laid low.
♋	Considerable debility as you advance in life!
♌	When the loss thou hast sustained is wearing off thy mind, the property will be accidentally recovered.
♍	A present is preparing for thee by the object of thy love.
♎	Thy condition will be greatly improved by marriage.
♏	The beauty, industry, and prudence of thy spouse will compensate for want of fortune.
♐	Much anxiety, and little advantage!
♑	News will soon arrive of the eruption of a volcano, which will cause great devastation.
♒	If the road of life be rugged in the outset, the termination will be smooth and pleasant.
♓	Thou shalt retain thy virginity for many years. A husband will at length take thee to his arms!

L.

One of them will shortly make you his heir.	♈
In a foreign land you will meet with many changes of fortune.	♉
A friend is about to present thee with a gift of great value.	♊
After you have passed the fifty-second year, expect a periodical visit of gout and rheumatism.	♋
Let thy search be still more minute than it has been.	♌
No opportunity is to be lost of forwarding thy suit; for a rival is about to reap all the fruits of thy attachment.	♍
You are in the way to great preferment.	♎
Thy bride will bring thee a large dowry; but thou shalt not enjoy much happiness with her, for she will be greatly afflicted with illness for many years.	♏
If, when you next behold the moon, it be at the full, you will be very fortunate; if it be not, you will be proportionally unsuccessful.	♐
A dreadful engagement by sea will soon take place.	♑
Your prosperity may be greatly augmented by care and circumspection.	♒
Thy husband will be both a glutton and a wine-bibber.	♓

LI.

♈	A secret enemy is calumniating thee to them; and, if care be not taken, he will cause a serious misunderstanding between you.
♉	In a foreign land thou shalt be under the sure and safe guidance of the celestial body which presides over thy destiny.
♊	The aspect of the Stars denotes destruction to thine enemies.
♋	You will be inclined to apoplexy; but due attention will prevent a fatal crisis.
♌	A discovery of the real truth will not be made during thy lifetime.
♍	Thy course of love shall be smooth; nothing can occur to disturb its harmony. Be happy: for thou hast reason to be so!
♎	You will have much success in business.
♏	Be not in haste to wed!—the demon of jealousy will be a constant inmate of your bosom.
♐	Failure!
♑	A man, at present in high power and authority, will speedily be debased.
♒	You will be the happy parent of a child of astonishing genius, and vast acquirements.
♓	Thou shalt wed a man whose genius and talents will procure him much respect and wealth.

LII.

A conspiracy among them is about to deprive thee of thy just rights.	♈
Relinquish all idea of going abroad: such a step would undoubtedly improve your fortune, but would as surely impair your health.	♉
Perseverance in the paths of virtue and honor will abash thine enemies; whilst thy friends, being knit closer to thee, will do all in their power to promote thy interests.	♊
A century of years is before thee; at their termination death will be a welcome visitor.	♋
It will be found when least expected.	♌
A rival is taking advantage of thy absence to ensnare the affections of thy beloved. Go to them; thy presence will put an end to their intercourse.	♍
Thou shalt be promoted to a post of great responsibility; and it will be well for thee if thou provest worthy of the trust.	♎
Thou art desirous to lose thy liberty; but, be assured, that thou shalt be as desirous to regain it.	♏
Disappointment and utter dismay!	♐
Ere many days pass, thou shalt appear before the judges of the land.	♑
A mingled texture of good and evil is the web which the Fates have woven for thee.	♒
In the choice of a husband, thou shalt be more happy than many of thy companions.	♓

THE ORACLE IS SILENT!

FOR

DARKNESS DOTH PREVAIL!

AND

THE CHILDREN OF MEN

ARE FORBIDDEN

TO INQUIRE FURTHER!!!

FORTUNE-TELLING BY CARDS.

In Fortune-telling by Cards—as in all games in which they are employed—the Ace ranks highest in value. Then comes the King, followed by the Queen, Knave, Ten, Nine, Eight, and Seven; these being generally the only cards used.

The order, and comparative value of the different suits, is as follows:—First on the list stand "Clubs," as they mostly portend happiness; and—no matter how numerous, or how accompanied—are rarely or never of bad augury. Next come "Hearts," which usually signify joy, liberality, or good temper; "Diamonds," on the contrary, denote delay, quarrels, and annoyance; and "Spades"—the worst suit of all—grief, sickness, and loss of money.

We are of course speaking generally, as, in many cases, the position of cards entirely changes their signification; their individual and relative meaning being often widely different. Thus, for example, the King of Hearts, the Nine of Hearts, and the Nine of Clubs, respectively signify, a liberal man, joy, and success in love; but change their position, by placing the King *between* the two nines, and you would read that a man, then rich and happy, would be ere long consigned to a prison!

SIGNIFICATION OF THE CARDS.

The individual meaning attached to the thirty-two cards employed is as follows:—

THE EIGHT CLUBS.

Ace of Clubs.—Signifies joy, money, or good news; if reversed, the joy will be of brief duration.

King of Clubs.—A frank, liberal man, fond of serving his friends; if reversed, he will meet with a disappointment.

Queen of Clubs.—An affectionate woman, but quick-tempered and touchy; if reversed, jealous and malicious.

Knave of Clubs.—A clever and enterprising young man; reversed, a harmless flirt and flatterer.

Ten of Clubs.—Fortune, success, or grandeur; reversed, want of success in some small matter.

Nine of Clubs.—Unexpected gain, or a legacy; reversed, some trifling present.

Eight of Clubs.—A dark person's affections, which, if returned, will be the cause of great prosperity; reversed, those of a fool, and attendant unhappiness, if reciprocated.

Seven of Clubs.—A small sum of money, or unexpectedly recovered debt; reversed, a yet smaller amount.

THE EIGHT HEARTS.

Ace of Hearts.—A love-letter, or some pleasant news; reversed, a friend's visit.

King of Hearts.—A fair liberal man; reversed, will meet with disappointment.

Queen of Hearts.—A mild, amiable woman; reversed, has been crossed in love.

Knave of Hearts.—A gay young bachelor, who dreams only of pleasure; reversed, a discontented military man.

Ten of Hearts.—Happiness, triumph; if reversed, some slight anxiety.

Nine of Hearts.—Joy, satisfaction, success; reversed, a passing chagrin.

Eight of Hearts.—A fair person's affections; reversed, indifference on his or her part.

Seven of Hearts.—Pleasant thoughts, tranquillity; reversed, ennui, weariness.

THE EIGHT DIAMONDS.

Ace of Diamonds.—A letter, soon to be received; and, if the card be reversed, containing bad news.

King of Diamonds.—A fair man—generally in the army—but both cunning and dangerous; if reversed, a threatened danger, caused by machinations on his part.

Queen of Diamonds.—An ill-bred, scandal-loving woman; if reversed, she is to be greatly feared.

Knave of Diamonds.—A tale-bearing servant, or unfaithful friend; if reversed, will be the cause of mischief.

Ten of Diamonds.—Journey, or change of residence; if reversed, it will not prove fortunate.

Nine of Diamonds.—Annoyance, delay; if reversed, either a family or a love quarrel.

Eight of Diamonds.—Love-making; if reversed, unsuccessful.

Seven of Diamonds.—Satire, mockery; reversed, a foolish scandal.

N. B.—In order to know whether the Ace, Ten, Nine, Eight, and Seven of Diamonds are reversed, it is better to make a small pencil-mark on each, to show which is the top of the card.

THE EIGHT SPADES.

Ace of Spades.—Pleasure; reversed, grief, bad news.
King of Spades.—The envious man, an enemy, or a dishonest law yer, who is to be feared; reversed, impotent malice.
Queen of Spades.—A widow; reversed, a dangerous and malicious woman.
Knave of Spades.—A dark, ill-bred young man; reversed, he is plotting some mischief.
Ten of Spades.—Tears, a prison; reversed, brief affliction.
Nine of Spades.—Tidings of a death; if reversed, it will be some near relative.
Eight of Spades.—Approaching illness; reversed, a marriage broken off, or offer refused.
Seven of Spades.—Slight annoyances; reversed, a foolish intrigue.

The Court cards of Hearts and Diamonds usually represent persons of fair complexion; Clubs and Spades, the opposite.

SIGNIFICATION OF DIFFERENT CARDS OF THE SAME DENOMINATION.

Four Aces, coming together, or following each other, announce danger, failure in business, and sometimes imprisonment. If one or more of them be reversed, the danger will be lessened, but that is all.
Three Aces, coming in the same manner.—Good tidings; if reversed, folly.
Two Aces.—A plot; if reversed, will not succeed.
Four Kings.—Rewards, dignities, honors; reversed, they will be less, but sooner received.
Three Kings.—A consultation on important business, the result of which will be highly satisfactory; if reversed, success will be doubtful.
Two Kings.—A partnership in business; if reversed, a dissolution of the same. Sometimes this only denotes friendly projects.
Four Queens.—Company, society; one or more reversed, denotes that the entertainment will not go off well.
Three Queens.—Friendly calls; reversed, chattering and scandal, or deceit.
Two Queens.—A meeting between friends; reversed, poverty, troubles, in which one will involve the other.
Four Knaves.—A noisy party—mostly young people; reversed, a drinking bout.
Three Knaves.—False friends; reversed, a quarrel with some low person.
Two Knaves.—Evil intentions; reversed, danger.
Four tens.—Great success in projected enterprises; reversed, the success will not be so brilliant, but still it will be sure.

Three tens.—Improper conduct; reversed, failure.
Two tens.—Change of trade or profession; reversed, denotes that the prospect is only a distant one.
Four nines.—A great surprise; reversed, a public dinner.
Three nines.—Joy, fortune, health; reversed, wealth lost by imprudence.
Two nines.—A little gain; reversed, trifling losses at cards.
Four eights.—A short journey; reversed, the return of a friend or relative.
Three eights.—Thoughts of marriage; reversed, folly, flirtation.
Two eights.—A brief love-dream; reversed, small pleasures and trifling pains.
Four sevens.—Intrigues among servants or low people, threats, snares, and disputes; reversed, that their malice will be impotent to harm, and that the punishment will fall on themselves.
Three sevens.—Sickness, premature old age; reversed, slight and brief indisposition.
Two sevens.—Levity; reversed, regret.

Any picture-card between two others of equal value—as two tens, two Aces, &c.—denotes that the person represented by that card runs the risk of a prison.

It requires no great efforts to commit these significations to memory, but it must be remembered that they are but what the alphabet is to the printed book; a little attention and practice, however, will soon enable the learner to form these mystic letters into words, and words into phrases; in other language, to assemble these cards together, and read the events, past and to come, their pictured faces pretend to reveal.

There are several ways of doing this; but we will give them all, one after another, so as to afford our readers an ample choice of methods of prying into futurity.

No. 1.—DEALING THE CARDS BY THREES.

Take the pack of thirty-two selected cards (viz., the Ace, King, Queen, Knave, Ten, Nine, Eight, and Seven of each suit), having before fixed upon the one you intend to represent yourself, supposing always you are making the essay on your own behalf. If not, it must represent the person for whom you are acting. In doing this, it is necessary to remember that the card chosen should be according to the complexion of the chooser, King or Queen of Diamonds for a very fair person, ditto of Hearts for one rather darker, Clubs for one darker still, and Spades only for one very dark indeed. The card chosen also loses its signification, and simply becomes the representative of a dark or fair man, or woman, as the case may be.

This point having been settled, shuffle the cards, and either cut them or have them cut for you (according to whether you are acting for yourself or another person), taking care to use the *left* hand. That done, turn them up by *threes*, and every time you find in these triplets *two of the same suit*, such as two Hearts, two Clubs, &c., withdraw the highest card and place it on the table before you. If the triplet should chance to be all of the same suit, the *highest* card is still to be the only one withdrawn; but should it consist of three of the *same value* but *different suits*, such as three Kings, &c., they are to be all appropriated. We will suppose that, after having turned up the cards three by three, you have been able to withdraw six, leaving twenty-six, which you shuffle and cut, and again turn up by threes, acting precisely as you did before, until you have obtained either *thirteen*, *fifteen*, or *seventeen* cards. Recollect that the number must always be uneven, and that the card representing the person for whom the essay is made must make one of it. Even if the requisite thirteen, fifteen, or seventeen have been obtained, and this one has not made its appearance, the operation must be recommenced. Let us suppose the person whose fortune is being read to be a lady, represented by the Queen of Hearts, and that fifteen cards have been obtained and laid out—in the form of a half circle—in the order they were drawn, viz., the Seven of Clubs, the Ten of Diamonds, the Seven of Hearts, the Knave of Clubs, the King of Diamonds, the Nine of Diamonds, the Ten of Hearts, the Queen of Spades, the Eight of Hearts, the Knave of Diamonds, the Queen of Hearts, the nine of Clubs, the Seven of Spades, the Ace of Clubs, the Eight of Spades. Having considered your cards, you will find among them two Queens, two Knaves, two tens, three sevens, two eights, and two nines; you are, therefore, able to announce:—

"The two Queens before me signify the reunion of friends; the two Knaves, that there is mischief being made between them. These two tens denote a change of profession, which, from one of them being between two sevens, I see will not be effected without some difficulty; the cause of which, according to these *three* sevens, will be illness. However, these two nines promise some small gain, resulting—so say these two eights—from a love-affair."

You now begin to count *seven cards, from right to left*, beginning with the Queen of Hearts, who represents the lady you are acting for. The seventh being the King of Diamonds, you may say:—

"You often think of a fair man in uniform."

The next seventh card (counting the King of Diamonds as *one*) proves to be the Ace of Clubs; you add:—

"You will receive from him some very joyful tidings; he, besides, intends making you a present."

Count the Ace of Clubs as "one," and proceeding to the next seventh card, the Queen of Spades, you resume:—

"A widow is endeavoring to injure you, on this very account; and" (the seventh card, counting the Queen as one, being the Ten of Diamonds) "the annoyance she gives you will oblige you to either take a journey or change your residence; but" (this Ten of Diamonds being imprisoned between two sevens) "your journey or removal will meet with some obstacle."

On proceeding to count as before, calling the Ten of Diamonds one, you will find the seventh card prove to be the Queen of Hearts herself, the person for whom you are acting, and may therefore safely conclude by saying:—

"But this you will overcome of yourself, without needing any one's aid or assistance."

Now take the two cards at either extremity of the half circle, which are, respectively, the Eight of Spades and the Seven of Clubs, unite them, and continue:—

"A sickness, which will lead to your receiving a small sum of money."

Repeat the same maneuver, which brings together the Ace of Clubs and the Ten of Diamonds:—

"Good news, which will make you decide on taking a journey, destined to prove a very happy one, and which will occasion you to receive a sum of money."

The next cards united, being the Seven of Spades and the Seven of Hearts, you say:—

"Tranquillity and peace of mind, followed by slight anxiety, quickly succeeded by love and happiness."

Then come the Nine of Clubs and the Knave of Clubs, foretelling:—"You will certainly receive money through the exertions of a clever dark young man—Queen of Hearts and King of Diamonds—which comes from the fair man in uniform; this rencontre announces some great happiness in store for you, and complete fulfillment of your wishes. Knave of Diamonds and Nine of Diamonds—Although this happy result will be delayed for a time, through some fair young man, not famed for his delicacy—Eight of Hearts and Ten of Hearts—love, joy, and triumph. The Queen of Spades, who remains alone, is the widow who is endeavoring to injure you, and who finds herself abandoned by all her friends!"

Now gather up the cards you have been using, shuffle and cut them with the left hand, and proceed to make them into three packs by dealing one to the left, one in the middle, and one to the right; a fourth is laid aside to form "a surprise." Then continue to deal the cards to each of the three packs in turn, until their number is exhausted, when it will be found that the left-hand and middle packs contain each five cards, whilst the one on the right hand consists of only four.

Now ask the person consulting you to select one of the three packs. We will suppose this to be the middle one, and that the cards comprising it are, the Knave of Diamonds, the King of Diamonds, the Seven of Spades, the Queen of Spades, and the Seven of Clubs. These, by recollecting our previous instructions regarding the individual and relative signification of the cards, are easily interpreted, as follows:—

"The Knave of Clubs—a fair young man, possessed of no delicacy of feeling, who seeks to injure—the King of Diamonds—a fair man in uniform—Seven of Spades—and will succeed in causing him some annoyance—the Queen of Spades—at the instigation of a spiteful woman—Seven of Clubs—but, by means of a small sum of money, matters will be finally easily arranged."

Next take up the left-hand pack, which is "for the house"—the former one having been for the lady herself. Supposing it to consist of the Queen of Hearts, the Knave of Clubs, the Eight of Hearts, the Nine of Diamonds, and the Ace of Clubs, they would read thus:—

"Queen of Hearts—the lady whose fortune is being told is, or soon will be, in a house—Knave of Clubs—where she will meet with a dark young man, who—Eight of Hearts—will entreat her assistance to forward his interests with a fair girl—Nine of Diamonds—he having met with delays and disappointment—Ace of Clubs—but a letter will arrive announcing the possession of money, which will remove all difficulties."

The third pack is "for those who did not expect it," and will be composed of four cards, let us say the Ten of Hearts, Nine of Clubs, Eight of Spades, and Ten of Diamonds, signifying:—

"The Ten of Hearts—An unexpected piece of good fortune and great happiness—Nine of Clubs—caused by an unlooked-for legacy—Eight of Spades—which joy may perhaps be followed by a slight sickness—Ten of Diamonds—the result of a fatiguing journey."

There now remains on the table only the card intended for the "surprise." This, however, must be left untouched, the other cards gathered up, shuffled, cut, and again laid out in three packs, not forgetting at the first deal to add a card to "the surprise." After the different packs have been duly examined and explained, as before described, they must again be gathered up, shuffled, &c., indeed, the whole operation repeated, after which the three cards forming "the surprise" are examined; and supposing them to be the Seven of Hearts, the Knave of Clubs, and the Queen of Spades, are to be thus interpreted:—

"Seven of Hearts—Pleasant thoughts and friendly intentions—Knave of Clubs—of a dark young man—relative to a malicious dark woman, or widow, who will cause him much unhappiness."

No. 2.—DEALING THE CARDS BY SEVENS.

After having shuffled the pack of thirty-two selected cards—which, as we before stated, consist of the Ace, King, Queen, Knave, Ten, Nine, Eight, and Seven of each suit—either cut them yourself, or, if acting for another person, let that person cut them, taking care to use the *left* hand. Then count seven cards, beginning with the one lying on the top of the pack. The first six are useless, so put them aside, and retain only the seventh, which is to be placed face uppermost on the table before you. Repeat this three times more, then shuffle and cut the cards you have thrown on one side, together with those remaining in your hand, and tell them out in sevens as before, until you have thus obtained twelve cards. It is, however, indispensable that the one representing the person whose fortune is being told should be among the number; therefore, the whole operation must be recommenced in case of it not having made its appearance. Your twelve cards being now spread out before you in the order in which they have come to hand, you may begin to explain them as described in the manner of dealing the cards in threes—always bearing in mind both their individual and relative signification. Thus, you first count the cards by sevens, beginning with the one representing the person for whom you are acting, going from *right* to *left*. Then take the two cards at either extremity of the line or half-circle, and unite them, and afterwards form the three heaps or packs and "the surprise" precisely as we have before described. Indeed, the only difference between the two methods is the manner in which the cards are obtained.

No. 3.—DEALING THE CARDS BY FIFTEENS.

After having well shuffled and cut the cards, or, as we have before said, had them cut, deal them out in two packs, containing sixteen cards in each. Desire the person consulting you to choose one of them;- lay aside the first card, to form "the surprise;" turn up the other fifteen, and range them in a half-circle before you, going from left to right, placing them in the order in which they come to hand, and taking care to remark whether the one representing the person for whom you are acting be among them. If not, the cards must be all gathered up, shuffled, cut, and dealt as before, and this must be repeated until the missing card makes its appearance in the pack chosen by the person it represents. Now proceed to explain them—first, by interpreting the meaning of any pairs, triplets, or quartettes among them; then by counting them in sevens, going from right to left, and beginning with the card representing the person consulting you; and lastly, by taking the cards at either extremity of the line and pairing them. This being done, gather up the fifteen cards, shuffle, cut, and deal them so as to form three packs of each five cards. From each of these three packs withdraw the topmost card, and place them on the one laid aside to form "the surprise," thus forming four packs of four cards each.

Desire the person for whom you are acting to choose one of these packs, "for herself" or "himself," as the case may be. Turn it up, and spread out the four cards it contains, from left to right, explaining their individual and relative signification. Next proceed in like manner with the pack on your left hand which will be "for the house;" then the third one, "for those who do not expect it;" and lastly, "the surprise."

In order to render our meaning perfectly clear, we will give another example. Let us suppose that the pack for the person consulting you is composed of the Knave of Hearts, the Ace of Diamonds, the Queen of Clubs, and the Eight of Spades *reversed*. By the aid of the list of meanings we have given, it will be easy to interpret them as follows:—

"The Knave of Hearts, is a gay young bachelor—the Ace of Diamonds—who has written, or will very soon write, a letter—the Queen of Clubs—to a dark woman—Eight of Spades reversed—to make proposals to her, which will not be accepted."

On looking back to the list of significations, it will be found to run thus:—

Knave of Hearts.—A gay young bachelor, who thinks only of pleasure.

Ace of Diamonds.—A letter, soon to be received.

Queen of Clubs.—An affectionate woman, but quick-tempered and touchy.

Eight of Spades.—If reversed, a marriage broken off, or offer refused.

It will thus be seen that each card forms, as it were, a phrase, from an assemblage of which nothing but a little practice is required to form complete sentences. Of this we will give a further example, by interpreting the signification of the three other packs—"for the house," ".for those who do not expect it," and "the surprise." The first of these, "for the house," we will suppose to consist of the Queen of Hearts, the Knave of Spades *reversed*, the Ace of Clubs, and the Nine of Diamonds, which reads thus:—

"The Queen of Hearts is a fair woman, mild and amiable in disposition who—Knave of Spades reversed—will be deceived by a dark, ill-bred young man—the Ace of Clubs—but she will receive some good news, which will console her—Nine of Diamonds—although it is probable that the news may be delayed."

The pack "for those who do not expect it," consisting of the Queen of Diamonds, the King of Spades, the Ace of Hearts *reversed*, and the Seven of Spades, would signify:—

"The Queen of Diamonds is a mischief-making woman—the King of Spades—who is in league with a dishonest lawyer—Ace of Hearts reversed—they will hold a consultation together—Seven of Spades—but the harm they will do will soon be repaired."

Last comes "the surprise," formed by, we will suppose, the Knave of Clubs, the Ten of Diamonds, the Queen of Spades, and the Nine of Spades, of which the interpretation is:—

"The Knave of Clubs is a clever, enterprising young man—Ten of Diamonds—about to undertake a journey—Queen of Spades—for the purpose of visiting a widow—Nine of Spades—but one or both of their lives will be endangered.

No. 4.—THE TWENTY-ONE CARDS.

After having shuffled the thirty-two cards, and cut, or had them cut, with the *left hand*, withdraw from the pack the first eleven, and lay them on one side. The remainder—twenty-one in all—are to be again shuffled and cut. That done, lay the topmost card on one side to form "the surprise," and range the remaining twenty before you, in the order in which they come to hand. Then look whether the card representing the person consulting you be among them; if not, one must be withdrawn from the eleven useless ones, and placed at the right extremity of the row; where it represents the missing card, no matter what it may really be. We will, however, suppose that the person wishing to make the essay is an officer in the army, and consequently represented by the King of Diamonds, and that the twenty cards ranged before you are, the Queen of Diamonds, the King of Clubs, the ten of Hearts, the Ace of Spades, the Queen of Hearts *reversed*, the Seven of Spades, the Knave of Diamonds, the Ten of Clubs, the King of Spades, the Eight of Diamonds, the King of Hearts, the Nine of Clubs, the Knave of Spades *reversed*, the Seven of Hearts, the Ten of Spades, the King of Diamonds, the Ace of Diamonds, the Seven of Clubs, the Nine of Hearts, the Ace of Clubs. You now proceed to examine the cards as they lay, and perceiving that all the four Kings are there, you can predict that great rewards await the person consulting you, and that he will gain great dignity and honor. The two Queens, one of them reversed, announce the reunion of two sorrowful friends; the three Aces, foretell good news; the two Knaves, one of them reversed, danger; the three tens, improper conduct.

You now begin to explain the cards, commencing with the first on the left hand, viz., the Queen of Diamonds. "The Queen of Diamonds, is a mischief-making, under-bred woman—the King of Clubs—endeavoring to win the affections of a worthy and estimable man—Ten of Hearts—over whose scruples she will triumph—Ace of Spades—the affair will make some noise—Queen of Hearts reversed—and greatly distress a charming fair woman who loves him—Seven of Spades—but her grief will not be of long duration. Knave of Diamonds—An unfaithful servant—Ten of Clubs—will make away with a considerable sum of money—King of Spades—and will be brought to trial—Eight of Diamonds—but saved from punishment through a woman's agency. King of Hearts—A fair man of liberal disposition—Nine of Clubs—will receive a large sum of money—Knave of Spades *reversed*—which will expose him to the malice of a dark youth of coarse manners. Seven of Hearts—pleasant thoughts, followed by—Ten of Spades—great chagrin—King of Diamonds—await a man in uniform, *who is the person consulting me*—Ace of Diamonds—but a letter he will speedily receive—Seven of Clubs—containing a small sum of money—Nine of Hearts—will restore his good spirits—Ace of Clubs—which will be further augmented, by some good news." Now turn up "the surprise"—which we will suppose to prove the Ace of Hearts—"a card that predicts great happiness, caused by a love-letter, but which making up the four Aces, shows that this sudden joy will be followed by great misfortunes."

Now gather up the cards, shuffle, cut, and form into three packs, at the first deal laying one aside to form "the surprise." By the time they are all dealt out, it will be found that the two first packets are each composed of seven cards, whilst the third contains only six.

Desire the person consulting you to select one of these, take it up, and spread out the cards, from *left* to *right*, explaining them as before described.

Gather up the cards again, shuffle, cut, form into three packs (dealing one card to the surprise), and proceed as before. Repeat the whole operation once more; then take up the three cards forming the surprise, and you then give their interpretation.

We may remark that no matter how the cards are dealt, whether by threes, sevens, fifteens, or twenty-one, when those lower than the Knave predominate, it foretells success; if Clubs are the most numerous, they predict gain, considerable fortune, &c.; if picture-cards, dignity and honor; Hearts, gladness, good news; Spades, death or sickness. These significations are necessarily very vague, and must of course be governed by the position of the cards.

THE ITALIAN METHOD.

Take a pack composed of thirty-two selected cards, viz., the Ace, King, Queen, Knave, Ten, Nine, Eight, and Seven of each suit. Shuffle them well, and either cut or have them cut for you, according to whether you are acting for yourself or another person. Turn up the cards by threes, and when the triplet is composed of cards of the same suit, lay it aside; when of three different suits, pass it by without withdrawing any of the three; but when composed of two of one suit and one of another, withdraw the highest card of the two. When you have come to the end of the pack, gather up all the cards except those you have withdrawn; shuffle, cut, and again turn up by threes. Repeat this operation until you have obtained fifteen cards, which must then be spread out before you, from *left* to *right*, in the order in which they come to hand.

Care must, however, be taken that the card representing the person making the essay is among them; if not, the whole operation must be recommenced until the desired result is obtained. We will suppose it to be some dark lady—represented by the Queen of Clubs—who is anxious to make the attempt for herself, and that the cards are laid out in the following order, from left to right:—Ten of Diamonds, Queen of Clubs, Eight of Hearts, Ace of Diamonds, Ten of Hearts, Seven of Clubs, King of Spades, Nine of Hearts, Knave of Spades, Ace of Clubs, Seven of Spades, Ten of Spades, Seven of Diamonds, Ace of Spades, Knave of Hearts.

On examining them, you will find that there are three Aces among them, announcing good news; but, as they are at some distance from each other, that the tidings may be some time before they arrive.

The three tens denote that the conduct of the person consulting the cards has not been always strictly correct. The two Knaves are enemies, and the three Sevens predict an illness, caused by them.

You now begin to count *five* cards, beginning with the Queen of Clubs, who represents the person consulting you. The fifth card, being the Seven of Clubs, announces that the lady will soon receive a small sum of money. The next fifth card proving to be the Ace of Clubs, signifies that this money will be accompanied by some very joyful tidings. Next comes the Ace of Spades, promising complete success to any projects undertaken by the person consulting the cards; then the Eight of Hearts, followed at the proper interval by the King of Spades, showing that the good news will excite the malice of a dishonest lawyer; but the Seven of Spades coming next, announces that the annoyance he can cause will be of short duration, and that a gay, fair young man—the Knave of Hearts—will soon console her for what she has suffered. The Ace of Diamonds tells that she will soon receive a letter from this fair young man—the Nine of Hearts—announcing a great success—Ten of Spades—but this will be followed by some slight chagrin—Ten of Diamonds—caused by a journey—Ten of Hearts—but it will soon pass, although—Knave of Spades—a bad, dark young man will endeavor—Seven of Diamonds—to turn her into ridicule. The Queen of Clubs, being representative of herself, shows that it is towards *her* that the dark young man's malice will be directed. Now take the cards at either extremity of the line, and pair them together. The two first being the Knave of Hearts and the Ten of Diamonds, you may say: "A gay young bachelor is preparing to take a journey—Ace of Spades and Queen of Clubs—which will bring him to the presence of the lady consulting the cards, and cause her great joy. Seven of Diamonds and Eight of Hearts—Scandal talked about a fair young girl. Ten of Spades and Ace of Diamonds—tears shed upon receipt of a letter. Seven of Spades and Ten of Hearts—great joy, mingled with slight sorrow. Seven of Clubs and Ace of Clubs—A letter promising money. Knave of Spades and King of Spades—the winning of a lawsuit. The Nine of Hearts, being the one card left, promises complete success."

Now gather up the cards, shuffle, cut, and deal them out in five packs—one for the lady herself, one for the house, one for "those who do not expect it," one for "those who do expect it," and one for "the surprise," in the first deal, laying one card aside for "consolation." The rest are then equally distributed among the other five packs, which will four of them contain three cards, whilst the last only consists of two.

We will suppose the first packet for the lady herself to be composed of the Ace of Diamonds, the Seven of Clubs, and the Ten of Hearts. The interpretation would run thus:—

"Ace of Diamonds—a letter will be shortly received—Seven of Clubs—announcing the arrival of a small sum of money—Ten of Hearts—and containing some very joyful tidings."

The second pack, " for the house," containing the King of Spades, the Nine of Hearts, and the Knave of Spades:—

"The person consulting the cards will receive a visit—King of Spades—from a lawyer—Nine of Hearts—which will greatly delight —Knave of Spades—a dark, ill-disposed young man."

The third pack, "for those who do not expect it," composed of the Ace of Spades, the Knave of Hearts, and the Ace of Clubs, would read:—

"Ace of Spades—pleasure in store for—Knave of Hearts—a gay young bachelor—Ace of Clubs—by means of money; but as the Knave of Hearts is placed between two Aces, it is evident that he runs a great risk of being imprisoned; and from the two cards signifying respectively 'pleasure' and 'money,' that it will be for having run into debt."

The fourth pack, "for those who do expect it," containing the Eight of Hearts, the Queen of Clubs, and the Ten of Diamonds:—

"The Eight of Hearts—the love-affairs of a fair young girl will oblige—the Queen of Clubs—the person consulting the cards—Ten of Diamonds—to take a journey."

The fifth pack, "for the surprise," consists of the Seven of Spades and the Ten of Spades, meaning:—

"Seven of Spades—slight trouble—Ten of Spades—caused by some person's imprisonment—The Card of Consolation—Seven of Diamonds—which will turn out to have been a mere report."

PRESENT, PAST, AND FUTURE.

The person wishing to try her fortune in this manner (we will suppose her to be a young, fair person, represented by the Eight of Hearts), must well shuffle, and cut with the left hand, the pack of thirty-two cards; after which she must lay aside the topmost and undermost cards, to form the surprise. There will now remain thirty cards, which must be dealt out in three parcels—one to the left, one in the middle, and one to the right.

The left-hand pack represents the Past; the middle, the Present; and the one on the right hand, the Future. She must commence with the "Past," which we will suppose to contain these ten cards: The King of Clubs, the Ace of Spades, the Knave of Diamonds, the Nine of Diamonds, the Ace of Hearts, the Knave of Hearts, the Queen of Hearts, the King of Spades, the Knave of Clubs, and the King of Hearts.

She would remark that picture-cards predominating was a favorable sign; also that the presence of three Kings proved that powerful persons were interesting themselves in her affairs. The three Knaves, however, warn her to beware of false friends, and the Nine of Diamonds predicts some great annoyance, overcome by some good and amiable person, represented by the Queen of Hearts. The two Aces also give notice of a plot. Taking the cards in the order they lay, the explanation would run thus:—

"The King of Clubs—a frank, open-hearted man—Ace of Spades—fond of gaiety and pleasure, is disliked by—Knave of Diamonds—an unfaithful friend—Nine of Diamonds—who seeks to injure him. The Ace of Hearts—a love-letter—Knave of Hearts—from a gay young bachelor to a fair, amiable woman—Queen of Hearts—causes—King of Spades—a lawyer to endeavor to injure a clever—Knave of Clubs—enterprising young man, who is saved from him by—the King of Hearts—a good and powerful man. Nevertheless, as the Knave of Clubs is placed between two similar cards, he has run great risk of being imprisoned through the machinations of his enemy."

The second parcel, "the Present," containing the Ten of Diamonds, the Nine of Spades, the Eight of Spades, the Queen of Diamonds, the Queen of Clubs, the Eight of Hearts, the Seven of Spades, the Ten of Spades, Queen of Spades, the Eight of Diamonds, signifies:—

"The Ten of Diamonds—a voyage or journey, at that moment taking place—Nine of Spades—caused by the death or dangerous illness of some one—Eight of Spades—whose state will occasion great grief—Queen of Diamonds—to a fair woman. The Queen of Clubs—An affectionate woman seeks to console—Eight of Hearts—a fair young girl, who is the person making the essay—Seven of Spades—who has secret griefs—Ten of Spades—causing her many tears—Queen of Spades—these are occasioned by the conduct of either a dark woman or a widow, who—Eight of Diamonds—is her rival."

The third packet of cards, "the Future," we will suppose to contain the Eight of Clubs, the Ten of Clubs, the Seven of Diamonds, the Ten of Hearts, the Seven of Clubs, the Nine of Hearts, the Ace of Diamonds, the Knave of Spades, the Seven of Hearts, the Nine of Clubs, which would read thus:—

"In the first place, the large number of small cards foretells success in enterprises, although the presence of three sevens predicts an illness. The Eight of Clubs—a dark young girl—Ten of Clubs—is about to inherit a large fortune—Seven of Diamonds—but her satirical disposition will destroy—Ten of Hearts—all her happiness. Seven of Clubs—A little money and—Nine of Hearts—much joy—Ace of Hearts—will be announced to the person making the essay by a letter, and—Knave of Spades—a wild young man—Seven of Hearts—will be overjoyed at receiving—Nine of Clubs—some unexpected tidings. The cards of surprise—viz., the King of Diamonds and the

Ace of Clubs—predict that a letter will be received from some military man, and that it will contain money."

THE STAR METHOD OF CONSULTING THE CARDS.

We will suppose the person making the essay to be a widow, and consequently represented by the Queen of Spades. This card is, therefore, to be withdrawn from the pack, and laid, face uppermost, upon the table. The remaining thirty-one cards are then to be well shuffled, cut, the topmost card withdrawn and placed lengthwise, and face uppermost, above the head of the Queen of Spades. The cards are to be shuffled, cut, and the topmost card withdrawn, twelve more times, the manner of their arrangement being this:—The Queen of Spades in the centre, the first card lengthwise above her head, the second ditto at her feet, the third on her right side, the fourth on her left, the fifth placed upright above the first, the sixth ditto below the second, the seventh at the right of the third, the eighth at the left of the fourth, the ninth, tenth, eleventh, and twelfth, at the four corners, and the thirteenth across the centre card—the Queen of Spades—thus forming a star. (See engraving on page 76.) We will suppose these fourteen cards to be the Queen of Spades, which represents the person making the essay; then—1. the Ace of Hearts; 2. the King of Clubs; 3. The Ten of Clubs: 4. Nine of Diamonds; 5. Queen of Clubs; 6. the Eight of Hearts; 7. the Ten of Spades; 8. the Knave of Clubs; 9. the Seven of Clubs; 10. the Ten of Hearts; 11. the Knave of Diamonds; 12. the Eight of Diamonds; 13. the Nine of Clubs. These being placed at right angles, the person consulting them takes them up two by two, beginning with those last laid down.

The first card, 12, the Eight of Diamonds, and the one in the *opposite* corner, viz., 11, the Knave of Diamonds, read—"Overtures will be made—Knave of Diamonds—by a fair young man—next two cards, 10 and 9, Ten of Hearts—which will prove unsuccessful—Seven of Clubs—on account of something connected with money. Next two cards, 8 and 7, the Knave of Clubs—a clever dark young man—Ten of Spades—will be greatly grieved by, 6—Eight of Hearts, a fair girl to whom he is attached. Next two cards, 5 and 4, the Queen of Clubs—A dark woman—Nine of Diamonds—will be annoyed at not receiving, 3—Ten of Clubs—a sum of money—nex two cards, 2 and 1, the King of Clubs—which was to have been sent her by a generous dark man, who is fond of obliging his friends—Ace of Hearts—it will at last arrive, accompanied by a love-letter—13th card, placed across the Queen of Spades, Nine of Clubs—and be the cause of unexpected gain to the person consulting the cards." There is a shorter and simpler way of doing this, by surrounding the card representing the person trying his or her fortune, with a less number of cards.

The cards are shuffled and cut as before described, and the topmost one withdrawn. We will suppose the centre card to be the

Knave of Clubs, representing a dark young man—the first topmost one proves to be the Ace of Clubs, and this is placed above the head of the Knave—the second, the Eight of Hearts, is placed at his feet—the third, the Knave of Diamonds, at his right side—the fourth, the Queen of Spades, on his left. These read—" Ace of Clubs—You

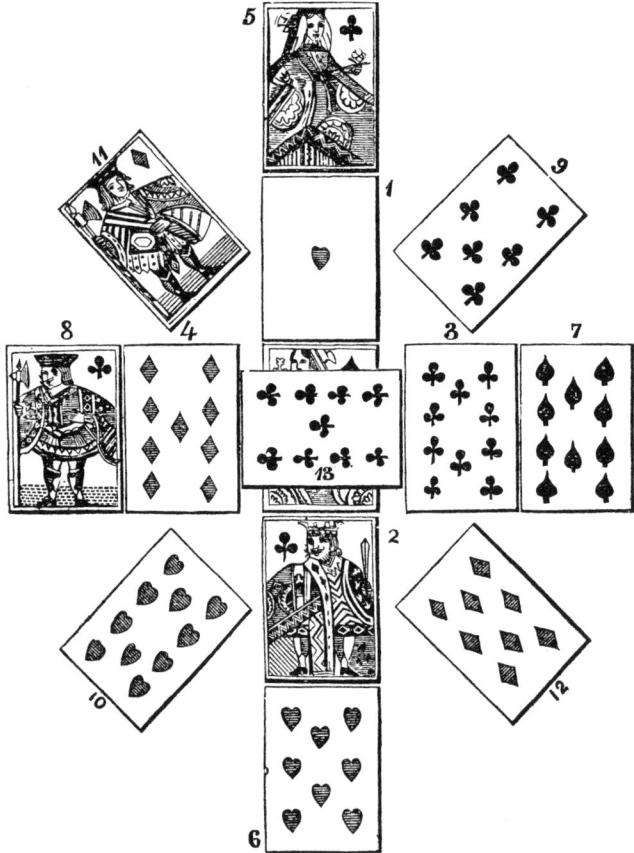

THE STAR METHOD OF CONSULTING THE CARDS.

will soon receive a letter, which will give you great pleasure—Eight of Hearts—from a fair girl. Knave of Diamonds—An unfaithful friend—Queen of Spades—and a malicious widow, will seek to injure you, on that very account."

TO KNOW IF YOU WILL GET YOUR WISH.

Shuffle the cards well, and cut, or have them cut, with the *left* hand. Then deal out thirteen cards. If among these is to be found one or more Aces, lay them aside, shuffle and cut the remaining ones, and again deal thirteen; withdraw the Aces as before, and again shuffle, cut, and deal. If, in these three deals, all four Aces make their appearance, you will get your wish. If all the Aces come at the first deal, the response is in the highest degree favorable

THE ENGLISH METHOD OF CONSULTING THE CARDS.

Having described the French and Italian methods of consulting the cards, we will proceed to notice the manner in which the art of fortune-telling is generally practiced in England and Scotland. Hitherto, only thirty-two cards have been made use of, but now the whole pack is employed. The significations also slightly differ; therefore we shall first give a complete list of them, and then pass on to describe how the cards are to be arranged, so as to disclose their mystic meanings.

Ace of Clubs.—Wealth, happiness, and peace of mind.
King of Clubs.—A dark man, upright, faithful, and affectionate in disposition.
Queen of Clubs.—A dark woman, gentle and pleasing.
Knave of Clubs.—A sincere, but hasty friend—also a dark man's thoughts.
Ten of Clubs.—Unexpected riches, and loss of a dear friend.
Nine of Clubs.—Disobedience to friends' wishes.
Eight of Clubs.—A covetous man—also warns against speculations.
Seven of Clubs.—Promises good fortune and happiness; but bids a person beware of the opposite sex.
Six of Clubs.—Predicts a lucrative business.
Five of Clubs.—A prudent marriage.
Four of Clubs.—Cautions against inconstancy or change of object for the sake of money.
Three of Clubs.—Shows that a person will be more than once married.
Two of Clubs.—A disappointment.
Ace of Diamonds.—A letter—from whom, and about what, is seen by the neighboring cards.
King of Diamonds—A fair man, hot-tempered, obstinate, and revengeful.
Queen of Diamonds.—A fair woman, fond of company, and a coquette.
Knave of Diamonds.—A near relation, who considers only his own interests. Also a fair person's thoughts.
Ten of Diamonds.—Money.
Nine of Diamonds.—Shows that a person is fond of roving

Eight of Diamonds.—A marriage late in life.
Seven of Diamonds.—Satire, evil speaking.
Six of Diamonds.—Early marriage and widowhood.
Five of Diamonds.—Unexpected news.
Four of Diamonds.—Trouble arising from unfaithful friends. Also a betrayed secret.
Three of Diamonds.—Quarrels, law-suits, and domestic disagreements.
Two of Diamonds.—An engagement, against the wishes of friends.
Ace of Hearts.—The house. If attended by Spades, it foretells quarreling—if by Hearts, affection and friendship—by Diamonds, money and distant friends—and Clubs, feasting and merry-making.
King of Hearts.—A fair man of good-natured disposition, but hasty and rash.
Queen of Hearts.—A fair woman, faithful, prudent, and affectionate.
Knave of Hearts.—The dearest friend of the consulting party. Also a fair person's thoughts.
Ten of Hearts.—Is prophetic of happiness and many children—is corrective of the bad tidings of cards next to it, and confirms good ones.
Nine of Hearts.—Wealth and high esteem. Also the wish card.
Eight of Hearts.—Pleasure, company.
Seven of Hearts.—A fickle and false friend, against whom be on your guard.
Six of Hearts.—A generous but credulous person.
Five of Hearts.—Troubles caused by unfounded jealousy.
Four of Hearts.—A person not easily won.
Three of Hearts.—Sorrow caused by a person's own imprudence.
Two of Hearts.—Great success; but equal care and attention needed to secure it.
Ace of Spades.—Great misfortune, spite.
King of Spades.—A dark, ambitious man.
Queen of Spades.—A malicious, dark woman—generally a widow.
Knave of Spades.—An indolent, envious person; a dark man's thoughts.
Ten of Spades.—Grief, imprisonment.
Nine of Spades.—A card of very bad import, foretelling sickness and misfortune.
Eight of Spades.—Warns a person to be cautious in his undertakings.
Seven of Spades.—Loss of a friend, attended with much trouble.
Six of Spades.—Wealth through industry.
Five of Spades.—Shows that a bad temper requires correcting.
Four of Spades.—Sickness.
Three of Spades.—A journey.
Two of Spades.—A removal.

Having given the signification of the various cards, we will now proceed to describe how they are to be employed. After having well shuffled, cut them three times, and lay them out in rows of nine cards each. Select any King or Queen you please to represent yourself; and wherever you find that card placed, count nine cards every way, reckoning it as one; and every ninth card will prove the prophetic one. Before, however, beginning to count, study well the disposition of the cards, according to their individual and relative signification. If a married woman consult the cards, she must make her husband the King of the same suit of which she is Queen; but if a single woman, she may make any favorite male friend King of whatever suit she pleases. As the Knaves of the various suits represent the *thoughts* of the persons represented by the picture-cards of a corresponding color, they should also be counted from.

TO TELL WHETHER YOU WILL GET YOUR WISH.

To try whether you will get your wish, shuffle the cards well, all the time keeping your thoughts fixed upon whatever wish you may have formed; cut them once, and remark what card you cut; shuffle them again, and deal out into three parcels. Examine each of these in turn, and if you find the card you turned up next either the one representing yourself—the Ace of Hearts or the Nine of Hearts—you will get your wish. If it be in the same parcel with any of these, without being next them, there is a chance of your wish coming to pass at some more distant period; but if the Nine of Spades makes its appearance, you may count on being disappointed.

FORTUNE-TELLING WITH DICE.

As answers to the innumerable questions which might be asked of the dice cannot be given in these pages, we annex a table of thirty-two questions, all of which are more or less interesting, especially to the young of either sex.

We will suppose a young lady, desiring to consult the dice, selects a question she wishes answered, takes two dice, and places them in the box. She shakes them three times, and, uttering the question aloud, throws them upon the table. She notes the number of spots upon the two dice, and looks after the corresponding answer in the table of answers.

If, for example, she has chosen question No. 5, "Does he think of me?" and she has thrown five and six, she will find page 99, and the answer No. 5 as follows: "Oh, yes, but with great bitterness." The process can be easily understood from this example.

TABLE OF QUESTIONS.

5 Does he think of me?
6 Will any one soon pay his addresses to me?

7. What must I do to please him?
8. Shall I answer?
9. Shall I grant what is asked of me?
10. How many admirers shall I have?
11. How many husbands shall I have?
12. What sort of a man will my husband be?
13. What does he think of me?
14. May I trust him?
15. Does he love me?
16. Does he think that I love him?
17. Will my heart remain free much longer?
18. Shall I soon get married?
19. Shall I experience many adventures?
20. Shall I be rich?
21. Will my secret be discovered?
22. Am I thought pretty?
23. Am I thought discreet, witty, interesting?
24. Will he ever become my husband?
25. Shall I do it?
26. Shall I see him soon again?
27. Shall I soon receive a letter?
28. Which of the two shall I choose?
29. Shall I soon receive a present?
30. Shall I soon take a journey?
31. Will my condition shortly be changed?
32. Will my wish be fulfilled?
33. What is he doing at present?
34. What will my husband be?
35. Will it prove a blessing to me?
36. Shall I soon receive the wished for tidings?

TABLE OF ANSWERS.

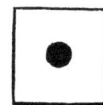

5. He thinks as much of you as you think of him.
6. To-morrow morning, about eleven o'clock.
7. Whatever you do, do it gracefully, and especially always make a very low curtsey to him.
8. Yes, but word the reply discreetly.
9. Oh no, you must not.
10. A dozen at least; sweet little angel, who would not adore you.
11. One.
12. Young, slender, and fair complexioned.
13. That you are a dear little creature.

14. No, you may not, for another such a scoundrel does not exist.
15. He cannot help himself.
16. You have let him see it plainly enough.
17. You know very well that it has not been free this long while.
18. In a week.
19. Your life will be peaceful as a quiet lake.
20. You will always have all you need.
21. It would be a good thing if it *were* discovered.
22. All except your nose, which is too short.
23. Discreet, indeed, but not witty, and interesting only at times.
24. Oh, no!
25. Why not?
26. To-morrow.
27. Not as soon as you would wish.
28. The one who has the longest nose.
29. Very soon, and it will be a kiss.
30. Yes, a very long one.
31. Yes, to your joy and happiness.
32. It will.
33. He is busy at his toilette, and at this very moment is curling his hair.
34. A rich young gentleman.
35. Yes, it will lead to the purest happiness.
36. Sooner than you expect.

 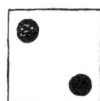

5. He does not in the least.
6. Unfortunately for you, much too soon.
7. Wear always a high-necked dress. Never appear with a bare neck, still less with bare arms—that he hates.
8. It is hazardous.
9. Yes, without the slightest fear.
10. As many admirers as you will have husbands.
11. Two—one squints.
12. Fat and round as a ball. He is exceedingly fond of sweet things, and is of a patient disposition.
13. That your glance has pierced his heart.
14. Have you not had proofs enough that he has the best heart in the world?
15. He is yours, heart and soul.
16. Oh no, he does not!
17. When you walk out to-morrow, note the first young gentleman you meet who bows to you—he is the one with whom you will soon fall in love.

18. In two years.
19. Your life will dash onward like a foaming torrent.
20. As rich as you are at present.
21. No, but it were advisable that you disclosed it as soon as possible.
22. When you are pleasant and friendly; but when under the influence of temper, you look hateful.
23. Neither very discreet nor very witty, but to *one* person, at least, very interesting.
24. If you will have him.
25. As you please, it will do no harm.
26. Before the autumn wind blows again over the meadow.
27. Yes, but not the one wished for.
28. He who most resembles a porcupine.
29. Yes, a bouquet.
30. You will soon behold cities which you never expected to visit.
31. When you shall wish it changed.
32. If it is really your wish.
33. He is examining his moustache to see how much it has grown during the night.
34. An engineer.
35. No, that is impossible.
36. Not so very soon.

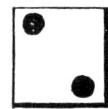 

5. Always. In sleep and in dreams, your dear image hovers about him. Even at the breakfast table he beholds your lovely countenance reflected from his buttered bread, and he eats it up for love.
6. Heaven help us! Are you not always surrounded with admirers?
7. Treat him always with frankness and candor, but never act coquettishly.
8. It were better not.
9. You might, but do it prudently.
10. Five—a lame man, a blind man, a deaf man, a dumb man, and a hunchback.
11. One, and a horribly jealous one, who will watch you with Argus' eyes.
12. Loving and tender; thirty kisses he will daily claim from you.
13. That, in fact, you are really hard-hearted.
14. At all events, you need not *mistrust* him so very much.
15. Does not his pale countenance betray his deep sorrow?
16. He hopes so, yet he often has doubts.

17. To-morrow afternoon, about five o'clock, Love's arrow will pierce your bosom.
18. In six weeks.
19. Many thrilling adventures.
20. Quite wealthy.
21. It will, unless you are every moment upon your guard.
22. Very pretty.
23 You are thought to be a good creature.
24. Yes.
25. If it will give you pleasure.
26. No, you are separated forever.
27. There is one now on the way.
28. The one who always gazes upon you with so shrewd an expression.
29. Yes, but it will come from a very different person from the one you think.
30. A short, sentimental one.
31. Yes, but you will be no better off for it.
32. If you do every thing in your power to promote it.
33. He is standing before the mirror, and thinks—"After all, my face is well enough, and my figure not bad."
34. A clergyman.
35. It will bring you both joy and sorrow.
36. Never.

5. Are not your eyes a pair of stars, which he who has once beheld can never forget?
6. Yes, my dear young lady; but be prudent, it is a sad rogue who will next pay attention to you.
7. Show a little more kindness toward human beings, and a little less toward cats.
8. Do so frankly and without affectation.
9. It would be too cruel to refuse.
10. One only, but one who will admire you more than all the rest of mankind together.
11. One, a fat little mushroom of a fellow.
12. Very ugly, but in your eyes handsomer than all the world beside—he has lost half a finger.
13. That it would be dangerous to trust you.
14. Oh yes, with your whole heart!
15. Do you not see how his cheek reddens, when he glances at you?
16. Without a doubt.

17. At the next ball, while dancing a cotillion, your heart will be touched.
18. Never.
19. Too many by far, especially love adventures.
20. You will possess so much wealth, that you will not know what to do with it.
21. It is discovered already.
22. Not beautiful, but very genteel.
23. You are thought to be a mischievous little vixen.
24. Yes, he, and several otners.
25. Do what you can not help doing.
26. Very soon.
27. The one you would like to receive, you will never receive.
28. The one with the heavy beard.
29. Very soon, a dear, sweet one!
30. Yes, and the one that you are looking forward to with such pleasure.
31. It will depend entirely upon yourself.
32. It will be, certainly.
33. He is drinking a glass of wine to the health of his dear one.
34. A lawyer.
35. It will bring you joy and happiness.
36. Perhaps not in a year yet.

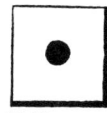 

5. He would like to, but he dare not.
6. When you cease your coquetry.
7. The next time you meet him give him your hand, and say. — "How amiable you are, sir, how handsome! in truth, I am exceedingly happy to be permitted to call you my friend."
8. It would never do to be silent, at any rate; give him a good reprimand.
9. You can not well do otherwise.
10. Two collegians, a tutor, and a captain in the army: perhaps also a fat old alderman.
11. One, and he will be the joy of your life.
12. Very tall, of a light brown complexion, wears spectacles, and is the essence of all that is noble, manly, and amiable.
13. That he can neither comprehend your behavior nor undei stand your words.
14. You may believe what *he* says, and not the world's tittle-tattle.
15. *That* you can find out when you next present him with a glass of water; if, in taking it, he tries to touch your hand, he loves you.

16. He thinks so, and is very much flattered by it.
17. At this moment your heart is not free—examine it.
18. In a year.
19. Very many, especially with rogues and robbers.
20. Rich in love, rich in all amiable and noble virtues, but not in money.
21. You think that it is a secret, but it never has been one.
22. You pass for it.
23. You are thought to be very capricious.
24. It is hardly possible.
25. It will be of no use, neither will it do you any harm.
26. If you write to him to come and see you, otherwise not.
27. Very soon, and oh, what a tender one!
28. The one who first reaches out his hand to you.
29. Yes, a living one.
30. A journey? yes, but not the one your thoughts are now dwelling upon.
31. Not so very soon.
32. Yes, but not as soon as you would like.
33. He is enjoying a refreshing slumber.
34. A physician.
35. So long only as you keep your heart pure and true, and without falsehood.
36. Yes, in a few hours.

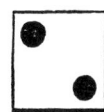 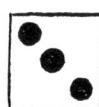

5. Heaven bless me! he has altogether too much to do; he has no time for such thoughts.
6. If you would treat a certain young gentleman with a little more regard, he would take pleasure in so doing.
7. Do not receive so much attention from others.
8. Answer him as such a letter deserves to be answered.
9. Ask your heart, and if it say yes, do you say yes likewise.
10. Your warmest admirers will always be boors.
11. One, a very stout fellow and very unpoetical.
12. Very tall and of a dark complexion; somewhat quarrelsome of a jealous disposition, rather rough, but always having the best intentions.
13. That it would be very dangerous to see you often.
14. Inquire what people say about him. True, there is much falsehood in what is rumored about him, yet something lies at the bottom of it.
15. With his whole heart and soul.
16. Since the last time he saw you, he is sure of it.

17. Who knows better than yourself that even now you are in love with him.
18. In five months.
19. Oh, no, very few.
20. You will have money; but, remember, money does not always make one rich, and seldom gives happiness, but is often poison to the heart, and the source of bitter woe.
21. If you tell it to no mortal, no.
22. If you could throw a little more repose into your features while you are speaking, you would be thought so.
23. You are thought to be a genius in every respect, but, for that very reason, you are thought to have many faults
24. Yes, he will.
25. Oh, by no means! what would people say?
26. At a time when you are the least expecting him.
27. Yes, and it will make you very happy.
28. The one who has the largest hand.
29. Not so very soon
30. Yes, the journey you are now thinking of.
31. Not in the way you wish.
32. Yes, and sooner than you expect.
33. He is at fisticuffs with his landlord.
34. A scientific man.
35. Certainly, although at first you will not be sensible of it.
36. Within three days, or never.

5. Certainly, quite often; as often, at least, as circumstances permit.
6. You will have wrinkles before that happens to you.
7. Do not be so dreadfully affected—let him see by your manners that you have a heart, that you are honest and sensible.
8. Answer just as your heart prompts you.
9. Be careful what you do; you might be very much laughed at for it.
10. Seven young officers, who will all blow out their brains on your account.
11. One, a dear, good, and amiable young man.
12. Amiable and cheerful, of a romantic turn, somewhat poetical good-hearted, although a little weak.
13. That you are the guiding star of his existence.
14. Look in his open, honest countenance, and you will see.
15. With ordinary Christian philanthropy, nothing more.

FORTUNE-TELLING WITH DICE.

16. If you cast such tender glances at him, as you did the last time you met, he can hardly doubt it.
17. Now you love one, and presently you will love another.
18. Within four years.
19. Your life will be a rather wearisome one.
20. If you take great pains, and are very economical.
21. There is one person who knows it, but he will not repeat it.
22. Some think you handsome, but others not.
23. You are thought to be a mere fashionable puppet, heartless and soulless.
24. You know yourself that it is impossible.
25. Think what your dear old mother would say
26. Yes, pretty soon.
27. Yes, but it will bring sad news.
28. The one who blushes oftenest.
29. You must be patient for a little while.
30. Not quite so soon as you wish or hope.
31. Very soon, and in an essential particular.
32. It will be fulfilled, but not completely, and not quite as you hope.
33. He is paying his addresses to an old woman
34. A merchant.
35. If you take it as Fortune means it.
36. In a month, perhaps.

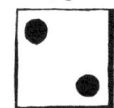 

5. Ah, you know very well that he does.
6. Yes, but only to make fun of you.
7. Do not put so much sugar in your coffee, or he will think you extravagant.
8. Perhaps you had better, unless you wish to mortify him.
9. Do it, certainly, if you can do it without blushing.
10. Two young students, one dark complexioned, one fair, one of whom will soon present you with a bouquet.
11. Five, and none of them good for any thing.
12. A little fellow, with a heavy beard, made up of conceit and vanity.
13. That you would be much more agreeable, if you were not so affected.
14. It is well to be prudent.
15. Oh yes, but you share his heart with others.
16. Not exactly, but he thinks that he could easily win your heart
17. For a year yet, but no longer
18. In six years—not sooner, though you may try ever so hard
19. Many adventures, but none interesting.

20. You will have more than a competence; but, if either you or your husband play at cards for money, you will lose it all.
21. You will betray it yourself.
22. Some few think you ugly, some pretty, and one thinks you beautiful.
23. You are thought to be quick at repartee, but none think you really witty.
24. Yes, if you succeed in winning his heart within two weeks.
25. Do it, but there is one person it will displease.
26. You will have to wait a while.
27. Yes, a very long one.
28. The modest little man.
29. Very soon, and one with which you will be much delighted.
30. Yes, and one that will cost you many tears.
31. Soon, and by an unexpected occurrence.
32. It will be, and more fully than you have reason to expect.
33. He is thinking about some witty speech that he will make when he is next in company.
34. A broker.
35. It will cost you many tears at first, but in the end all will go well.
36. Very soon

5. He is thinking of you now, and very tenderly.
6. A number, and two or three at the same time.
7. Dress your hair neatly, do not wink so much, sit erect, and be polite to everybody.
8. Place a poppy beneath your pillow to-night, and you will dream what you ought to do.
9. What will a certain person say to it?
10. A dried-up old bachelor whom you can not endure.
11. Two—a rickety old fellow, and a wild young man.
12. A man of strong character—energetic and high-minded, with wit and humor also.
13. That you have broken his heart.
14. No one deserves confidence better than he does.
15. He is a true friend to you, that is all.
16. He has never thought about it at all.
17. As to your heart, that will be free enough always.
18. Very soon
19. Many, and many of them interesting ones.
20. If you keep from speculating.

21. If you can keep it a secret yourself, but you are too much given to blabbing.
22. If you did not wrinkle your nose when you laugh, you would be thought very pretty.
23. You are thought by some very peculiar—there is only one person who really understands you.
24. If you can love him truly.
25. Yes, it will cause you much pleasure.
26. Not until you have both gray hairs.
27. Not so very soon, but then it will be a very tender one.
28. The most unpretending one.
29. At present no one thinks of giving you any thing.
30. One which will give you much pleasure.
31. Soon, and in a way you never could have dreamed of.
32. Sooner than you expect.
33. He is sighing over the low state of his purse.
34. A farmer.
35. If you are always prudent, thoughtful, and cheerful.
36. You know when you have reason to expect it.

5. He does; but he will, at some future day, be sorry for it.
6. My dear young lady, congratulate yourself if they do not, for few are worth having.
7. Be not so sentimental, and do not talk so much about poetry and the tender feelings, but show a little practical common sense.
8. What is spoken vanishes, what is written remains.
9. You may grant every thing that he asks, for he will ask nothing unworthy of you.
10. Five and twenty—all nice, handsome young gentlemen, five of whom are in love with you already.
11. Three very respectable gentlemen.
12. A horrible fellow—big as a barn door, and in love with himself, because nobody else is.
13. He thinks that you would like to bring him to despair.
14. You would do well to consult your best female friend about it.
15. His heart has long been another's, and to her he will never be unfaithful.
16. Oh, no, but he thinks how pleasant it would be if you did love him.
17. Your heart is free at present, but will not be so long.
18. Not until you love a certain person more tenderly than you do at this moment.

19. Yes, and you will in vain sigh for repose.
20. As long as you make good use of your money; if you cease to do this, your wealth will vanish into air.
21. No, it will not.
22. If you dress your hair plainly, and wear a dark dress, with rose-colored ribbons.
23. Discreet, but very vain and proud.
24. Certainly, if he is not already engaged.
25. Of course, you would be a fool if you did not.
26. Not so very soon.
27. Yes, but the paper has been wet with many tears.
28. The one with the big ears.
29. Some one would like to make you a present, but you will do well not to accept it.
30. An important and joyful occurrence will prevent it.
31. Not so very soon.
32. That will depend upon your own conduct—it will, if you act prudently.
33. He is about to hasten to your presence.
34. A letter-carrier.
35. If you do not for an instant lose your presence of mind.
36. Not so very quickly.

5. Dear creature, he adores you.
6. Yes, but it will not conduce to your happiness.
7. Enjoy your life; be pleasant and gay, like the birds in May.
8. Do so without hesitation.
9. Ask your mother for advice; in such matters she understands what is best.
10. Two—but one has only one eye, and the other has no nose.
11. Only one.
12. Young and handsome, with rosy cheeks; he loves you heartily, and will do any thing to please you.
13. He thinks that you have been deceiving him, and can not conceive for what purpose.
14. Ask some one older than yourself—some female friend.
15. His heart was yours from the first moment that you met.
16. He thinks at least that you would like to have him love *you*.
17. The next journey you take, you will fall in love.
18. Within two years.
19. Some pleasant ones, and kind friends will protect you from unpleasant ones.
20. No, never.

21. Nobody thinks of inquiring about it.
22. Rather pretty, but without any expression of countenance.
23. You are thought to be the most charming character in the world.
24. He would, if it were not for a certain false friend.
25. Certainly, you can not do better.
26. He is now thinking how to bring about an interview as soon as possible.
27. You will shortly receive a very foolish one.
28. The one with a large mouth.
29. A splendid present, and very shortly.
30. You will have an opportunity to take a journey, but you will not take advantage of it.
31. Yes, and in the way you are now thinking of.
32. It will be your own fault if it is not.
33. He is practicing a speech before the glass.
34. A bookseller.
35. It will be a prelude to the fulfillment of your warmest wishes.
36. You will soon receive it, and shed tears of joy.

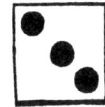 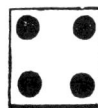

5. He thinks of you, but not in the way you would like to have him.
6. Twenty charming young officers will flock around you within the next two weeks.
7. Walk in the sun without your hat, until you are tanned yellow as an orange.
8. Yes, but give him a good reprimand, for he deserves it.
9. Not wholly, but it part.
10. Fifty, at least, but they are all ugly as sin.
11. Twenty-five, if you take all that offer.
12. Crooked and lame, and as thin as a bean-pole.
13. He thinks: "I will tear your image from my heart, for you do not deserve my love."
14. Heartily and frankly.
15. He loves you, but he resists his passion with all his might, because he does not think he is loved in return.
16. Not that you love him, but that you are a little smitten with him.
17. It will be a long time before you give away your heart, you prude.
18. Within a year.
19. No.
20. Gold will rain down upon you.

92 FORTUNE-TELLING WITH DICE.

21. You had better be upon your guard, for something of it has leaked out already.
22. Lay aside your affectation—do not laugh so loud and shrill that you make a person's ears ache, and then you will be quite pretty.
23. You are thought good-natured enough, but vain and silly.
24. If you would flirt less with those young officers, he would gladly be your husband.
25. People will laugh at you, but let not that prevent you.
26. It must be altogether by accident, if at all, for he has sworn never to see you again.
27. You will receive one very soon, but it will be perfectly incomprehensible to you.
28. The one who will soon say to you—"Yes, lady, yes, I swear it!"
29. Yes, one with which you will be much delighted.
30. A sad occurrence will prevent your expected journey.
31. Yes, but not in the way you expect.
32. Wicked people will prevent its fulfillment.
33. He is gaping and thinking to himself: "How dull and tiresome is life."
34. A literary man.
35. It will at first give you much pleasure, but afterward it will cost you a few tears.
36. You will soon receive it, and from one—yes, *one*—and does not your heart tell you who that one is?

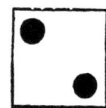 

5. At this moment he is resting his head in his hand, while your image rises to his view.
6. Yes, a bull-dog looking fellow.
7. Pay him a little more attention, and, the next time you meet, take a seat at his right side, and be careful to eat no cheese.
8. Answer what your heart dictates.
9. No, let him pine.
10. Just a dozen, but all old fellows, who have long ago passed the spring-time of life.
11. One possibly, but perhaps none.
12. A great favorite at balls and parties, the darling of all the ladies, and yours above all.
13. He thinks: "Why does she always look so coldly upon me? Is it that she can not endure me?"
14. Has he ever deceived you, that you should distrust him?
15. With pain and longing.
16. He thought so once, but he thinks so no longer

17. In about six weeks, by starlight, your heart will be softened.
18. In a year or two.
19. A reasonable quantity.
20. Labor always to be rich in discretion and contentedness of mind.
21. It is half discovered already.
22. Stately and beautiful, like a young queen.
23. You are thought original in every respect.
24. No, you need not expect that.
25. If you do not, you are lost.
26. In a few weeks.
27. Yes, in eight days.
28. The one who shortly presents you with a flower.
29. A present which you will soon wish you had never accepted.
30. Soon, and in the company of a young gentleman.
31. In a very agreeable manner.
32. An unexpected accident will prevent its accomplishment.
33. He is fastening his wrist-bands.
34. A man of business.
35. If you are strong enough to repress all pride and vanity on its account, it will prove one.
36. Not so soon as you wish, and other unpleasant tidings will come with it.

5. More than you think of *him.*
6. No one worth the having, only a sentimental drover.
7. You must not eat so heartily.
8. There can be no danger in it, at any rate.
9. You would rejoice one heart, and break two—would you do that?
10. Two, a handsome clerk, and a still handsomer young lawyer.
11. One, and you will find him one too many.
12. An old drunkard, and a gambler.
13. He thinks: "She has caused me so much suffering that I can never forgive her."
14. Trust him, but still keep your eyes open.
15. He loves you as much as he can, but he can not love you very much.
16. No, but he thinks you wish him well, as a sister does a brother.
17. Is your heart your own *now?*
18. In three years.
19. Mischievous persons will prepare many for you.
20. You will have gold pieces by the bushel.

21. If you act discreetly, it will not.
22. You roll your eyes about too much, and your ears are ill shaped, but your hand is beautiful, and your feet are like a fairy's.
23. You are thought a little foolish, yet prudent enough, and at times somewhat witty and interesting.
24. You do not wish him to be, and he does not wish to be.
25. If you are prudent, it can do no harm.
26. Next fall.
27. Not the one you wish—*that* will be delayed a little.
28. The noble-looking one, who is so polite and courteous in his manner.
29. A present, over which you will shed tears of joy.
30. Very soon, and in pleasant company.
31. Yes, and exactly to your wishes.
32. It will, and to your infinite happiness.
33. He is daubing his hair with pomatum.
34. A mechanic—probably a ship-builder.
35. All that happens to us happens as a blessing, but we often misinterpret it.
36. Do not be impatient—they will not come so very quickly.

5. You can not expect that of him, for he never thinks.
6. The first person who meets you to-morrow morning will, from that hour, be your admirer.
7. Fall out with him a little, but never let it be in earnest.
8. If you have discretion enough, answer.
9. Tell your brother the whole affair, and hear what he says. Brothers judge correctly in such cases.
10. One a stupid little fellow, with yellow hair, and a mouth that stretches from ear to ear.
11. As many as you have had lovers.
12. Handsome and well-formed, in the prime of life.
13. That you are a pretty little creature, but much too coquettish.
14. Trust no one blindly in this world.
15. If he could hope to find a return, he would gladly love you.
16. He thinks you are almost dying for love of him.
17. You have been twenty times in love already, and you will be so twenty times more.
18. In three or four years.
19. Storms and calms, as is the way in this world.
20. You will never suffer want, if you are always industrious.
21. No, but by keeping it secret you will bring upon yourself many disagreeable consequences.

22. Year a more cheerful countenance, and you would be really beautiful, but an ill-humored expression destroys the prettiest face.
23. Witty and amusing.
24. If he is not your husband, it will be your own fault.
25. Do it, but without much noise.
26. At the next party you are at.
27. If you expect a letter from him, you need not hope for it very soon ; he is angry, and it will be long before he forgives you.
28. The one with the pig's eyes.
29. Very soon, and from one you love.
30. Very shortly, and one which will have a decisive influence upon your whole life.
31. If you act prudently in a critical moment which is near at hand, it will.
32. Yes, but to your misfortune.
33. He is writing a love-letter.
34. An alderman.
35. If it happens of itself, without your interference, it will be the cause of much happiness to you.
36. It will come some day, but not soon.

5 As one thinks of a little, insignificant creature.
6 Yes, a sailor will pay you attention, but this sailor is a rich man's son, who has run away from home to follow the sea.
7. Do what he asks of you the next time you meet.
8. For heaven's sake, no, it will turn out badly for you both.
9. It were better you should not, although it would do no great harm.
10. A rich young planter, and two students.
11. One whom you will have completely under your thumb.
12. A phlegmatic old fellow, who will almost weary the life out of you.
13. That you are pretty and good, and that, if he could love anybody, it would be you.
14. He likes to flirt, but toward you his intentions are honorable.
15. You are his first and his last love.
16. He imagines it possible, at times, because he wishes it so much.
17. For two years yet; do not wish it otherwise.
18. In five years.
19. When you are traveling—not at other times.

20. If you always save up your pennies.
21. There is nothing hid so carefully, but it comes to light at last.
22. You are thought to be a master-piece of heaven's workmanship.
23. Somewhat thoughtless, but good at heart, and of a clear understanding.
24. He will be, and you will live happily together.
25. There is danger in it certainly, but, if you are very prudent, it may prove fortunate.
26. He will pay you a visit this very day.
27. Not before you have written one.
28. The one who shall first confess or has already confessed his love for you.
29. Yes, and from a person whom you can not endure.
30. If you wish to, you will have an opportunity.
31. No, not for a long time.
32. Yes, but it will break one person's heart.
33. He is just overturning his inkstand on the table, and he is not a little startled at it.
34. A wealthy country gentleman.
35. Yes.
36. This very day.

5. You are in his thoughts by day, and in his dreams by night.
6. Not in two years yet.
7. Be gentle as a dove, and patient as a lamb—he can not bear to be opposed or contradicted.
8. That is now a matter of indifference—tears must flow whether you answer or not.
9. If you do, it is much to be feared that, sooner or later, you will greatly regret it.
10. One, a young speculator, tall, slender, and handsome, with black hair and eyes—in short, a paragon.
11. One, a real domestic tyrant.
12. Dry as a herring, and very gluttonous.
13. That you are still quite childish, and without discretion.
14. You would mortify him deeply, if you did not.
15. You can not think to what extent; you should see the tender verses that he daily writes about you.
16. He thinks that all the ladies are in love with him; and you, of course, among the rest.
17. You will fall in love very soon, but it will cost you many tears.
18. In five or six years.
19. Many, especially when you attend balls.

20. Not very.
21. Not for a while.
22. That you have a sweet, angelic face—there is nothing more charming to be seen.
23. Possibly so.
24. He would be, if a bitter enemy did not stand between you, and separate you for this world.
25. It will cost you many tears, if you do it, but there will be tears of joy among them.
26. If you visit him—he is displeased, and will not visit you.
27. Your correspondents are all occupied with other matters.
28. The one who will stumble when dancing with you at the next ball.
29. Yes, but a somewhat insignificant one.
30. You will not want for invitations; if you wish it, you will be able to take many journeys.
31. Not in any matter of importance.
32. Yes, but it will make you many enemies.
33. He is railing at his tailor, who will not trust him any longer.
34. A military man.
35. No.
36. To-morrow, probably, but if not, next week.

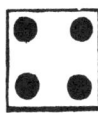 

5. As a person thinks of one with whom he is greatly pleased.
6. Why do you ask? they are all on their knees before you already.
7. Always wear a bouquet of flowers on your bosom, but never in your hair, and the next time you meet him, place a forget-me-not in his button-hole.
8. Reflect, my dear young lady, what that might lead to in the end.
9. Do so, with a careless air, and no harm will come of it.
10. In the first place, a little inspector, in the second, a young merchant, the nicest of his kind.
11. One short, one tall, and one of middle stature.
12. Hump-backed, and with a nose as long as your arm.
13. He has always thought you an angel, now he sees that you have a little of the d—l in you.
14. Trust him as long as you can without mistrusting others.
15. Without you all would be darkness in his soul—you are his sun, his moon, your eyes are his stars.
16. Yes, but he thinks that you love others besides him.
17. Very soon you will fall in love with a person that you now can not endure.

18. In seven years.
19. Many, and when you least expect it.
20. For a short time—your own indiscretion will impoverish you.
21. No.
22. When you droop your head, at times, so gracefully, and cast your eyes so prettily to the ground, you are enchanting.
23. No one can venture to dispute that you are the most charming, the most discreet, and the wittiest of mortals.
24. Yes, but you will live rather uncomfortably with him.
25. Alas, it is quite indifferent.
26. He has taken some offense, and for the present will not come.
27. Very soon, a dear, sweet letter.
28. The stoutest.
29. Not for some time.
30. A very, very long one.
31. When the time comes that you wish it.
32. Yes, but it will excite the envy of a certain person, and that will sadden your joy.
33. He is eating buckwheat cakes and sausages.
34. A naval officer.
35. A blessing to you and a delight to your friends.
36. Not the wished for, but very different tidings.

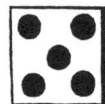 

5. Not yet, he will perhaps when he has seen you oftener.
6. There is one who is already paying attention to you, but he does it so awkwardly that you do not remark it.
7. If you were to do wonders to please him, he would still see something in you to find fault with.
8. Reflect whether it would be proper.
9. If it will give you pleasure, do so; no one will laugh at you for it.
10. A young merchant, William by name, and two students beside.
11. One, a person whom you already know and love—his name begins with a J.
12. A very funny fellow, full of all sorts of tricks.
13. He thinks: "If I only knew what to do to gain her favor!"
14. Prove him carefully first.
15. In secret, but he will never venture to let any one perceive it.
16. He thinks so, still he fears your inconstancy.
17. Your heart is not your own at present, but it will soon be free again.
18. This very year.
19. Very soon, a very interesting one.

20. Yes, but if you are not very prudent you will lose all again.
21. Yes, soon.
22. In the evening, when you are the queen of the ball, you are more beautiful than a fairy, for then you strive to shine but at other times, when you wear your everyday face, you are quite ugly.
23. You are sometimes really silly, but people pardon that in you, for understanding only comes with years.
24. No, he will never marry.
25. Do it, if you take a real pleasure in it.
26. You have too deeply offended him; he will never see you again.
27. In a few days—the most interesting you have ever received.
28. The one who titters the most.
29. Perhaps to-morrow—yet there may be some delay.
30. Just imagine it—a journey to Africa!
31. Somewhat, and agreeably.
32. That will depend upon your behavior.
33. He is sipping a glass of wine, and saying, "How very fine!"
34. A surgeon.
35. It will, at least, cause you many happy hours.
36. If you do not take some pains, never.

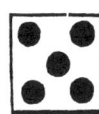 

5. Oh yes, but with great bitterness.
6. The person who first presents you with a flower will soon pay his addresses to you.
7. Do what you will, it is labor lost, for he is a great fault-finder
8. At least, wait for another letter before you answer.
9. If you do so, the person who now asks it of you will be the first to laugh at you.
10. A young, handsome, slender fellow, called Robert, besides one of your cousins.
11. One, the person whom you now think of the least.
12. A real good-for-nothing, who will give you trouble enough, yet a dear fellow.
13. He thinks: "I do not know what it means, yet she has looked very tenderly at me for some time past."
14. Too much confidence has deceived many a one.
15. Truly and faithfully—you are the sole object of his wishes; to gain your hand, he is laboring in the sweat of his brow.
16. He is much too jealous to be confident of it.
17. Some one will but too soon rob you of your heart and your repose.

18. When the roses bloom again.
19. Not at present, but in course of time.
20. You could become so, if you were resolved upon it.
21. You have nothing to fear.
22. Only in the presence of your lover can you be thought pretty, but then a heavenly angel looks out of your eyes, bathes you in sunshine, and you yourself become an angel.
23. Your heart is pure, your mind clear, and your soul devout.
24. Of course, who else should ever be?
25. Reflect first whether there is not one heart which you would deeply wound by doing it.
26. Very unexpectedly—next month.
27. Early to-morrow morning.
28. The one with a snub nose.
29. Yes, very soon.
30. A delightful journey westward.
31. Not so soon as you expect, nor in the way that you expect.
32. If you wish it very much.
33. He is reading a letter.
34. A carpenter.
35. It is extremely doubtful.
36. Very soon, but all your expectations will not be gratified.

5. He does not venture, for when he does his heart throbs to bursting.
6. Yes, an old gentleman with a wooden leg will soon do so.
7. Let him see that you love him, and prove it to him by sending him a handsome pocket-book.
8. Yes, in a cheerful, jesting style.
9. It would be a step which would have important consequences, yet it will depend upon yourself whether they will be fortunate or unfortunate.
10. In the first place, all your cousins love you, and then a person whom you can not bear—his name begins with an F.
11. However many you may have, it would be better that you had none.
12. Handsome as an Adonis, and a genius—you are his beau ideal, as he is yours.
13. If she were not so sentimental, she would please me.
14. Whom would you trust, if not him?
15. Just as much as you love him.
16. As often as he sees you, he thinks to himself: "No, she does not love me, she can not love me!"

17. Do you not already love as tenderly as one can love?
18. When puss lays an egg.
19. You are so imprudent that it can not be otherwise.
20. You will always have as much as you have at present.
21. Among your friends there is a Judas who will discover and betray it.
22. You are like a flower, so beautiful, so sweet, so pure!
23. You are thought very artless, the rest time must develop.
24. Do not loose your hold upon him; in the end he must surrender.
25. If you can without blushing.
26. When the spring comes again.
27. In a few weeks, the one longed for.
28. The one who first says: "We met by chance."
29. Some one is thinking about making you one, but it is not certain that any thing will come of it.
30. Yes, to Europe.
31. Very soon.
32. Not entirely.
33. He is kissing a trifling keepsake of yours.
34. An artist or a lieutenant.
35. It will render you very happy.
36. Very soon, and more agreeable than you expect.

GOOD AND BAD OMENS.

The word omen is well known to signify a sign, good or bad, or a prognostic. It may be defined to be that indication of something future which we get as it were by accident, and without seeking for. A superstitious regard to omens seems anciently to have made very considerable additions to the common load of infelicity. They are in these enlightened days pretty generally disregarded, and we look back with perfect security and indifference on those trivial and truly ridiculous accidents which alternately afforded matter of joy and sorrow to our ancestors. Omens appear to have been so numerous that we must despair of ever being able to recover one-half of them and to evince that in all ages men have been self-tormentors, the bad omens fill a catalogue infinitely more extensive than that of the good. An extensive set of omens has been taken from what first happens to one, or what animal or person one meets first in the morning, or at the commencement of an undertaking—the *first-foot*, as it is called. To stumble has been universally held to presage misfortune. Some semblance of a reason might be found for this belief, inasmuch as stumbling may be supposed to indicate that that self-possession and conscious courage, which are in themselves half a victory over circumstances, are lacking—the want of them, therefore, being half a defeat; but in most cases the interpretation seems altogether arbitrary. The dread of a hare crossing the path seems to be widely prevalent; while to see a wolf is a good omen. This feeling is probably a remnant of warlike times, when the timid hare suggested thoughts of cowardice and flight; while the bold wolf, sacred to Odin, was emblematic of victory. The character of the hare for being unlucky is also connected with the deep-rooted belief that witches are in the habit of transforming themselves into hares. That to meet an old woman is unlucky, is another very general belief; arising, without doubt, from the same causes that led to their being considered witches. In some places, women in general are unlucky as first-foot, with the singular exception of women of bad reputation. This belief prevailed as far back as the age of Chrysostom. Priests, too, are ominous of evil. If hunters of old met a priest or friar, they coupled up their hounds and went home in despair of any further sport that day. This superstition seems to have died out, except in the case of sailors, who still consider the clergy a "kittle cargo," as a Scotch skipper expressed it, and anticipate a storm or mischance when they have a black coat on board. This seems as old as the prophet Jonah. Sneezing, likewise, has long been looked upon as supernatural, for this reason, that it is sudden, unaccountable, uncontrollable, and therefore ominous. The person is considered as possessed for the time, and a form of exorcism is used. A nurse would not think she had done her duty, if, when her charge sneezes, she did not say, "Bless the child," just as the Greeks, more than two thousand years ago, said, "Zeus protect thee."

One general remark, however, it is important to make in regard to omens. An omen is not conceived to be a mere sign of what is destined to be—it is conceived as causing, in some mysterious way, the event it forebodes; and the consequence, it is thought, may be prevented by some counteracting charm. Thus the spilling of salt not only forebodes strife, but strife is conceived as the consequence of the spilling of the salt, and may be hindered by taking up the spilled salt, and throwing it over the left shoulder. Perhaps half the superstitious beliefs that yet survive among civilized and Christian communities group themselves round the subject of love and marriage—of such intense interest to all, yet so mysterious in its origin, and problematic in its issue. The liking or passion for one individual rather than any other is so unaccountable, that the God of Love has been fabled blind: it is of the nature of fascination, magic, spell. And then, whether happiness or the reverse shall be the result, seems beyond the reach of ordinary calculation. All is apparently given over to mystery, chance, fortune; and any circumstances may, for what we know, influence or indicate what fortune's wheel shall bring round. Hence the innumerable ways of prognosticating which of two or more persons shall be first married, who or what manner of person shall be the future husband or wife, the number of children, &c. It is generally at particular seasons, as at the Eve of St. Agnes, and Halloween, that the vail of the future may thus be lifted.

The observation of *lucky* and *unlucky* days was once an important matter, and was often the turning-point of great events. It is now mostly confined to the one subject of marriage. In fixing the wedding day, May among months and Friday among days are shunned by many people, both in educated and uneducated circles; for in this matter, which is the exclusive province of women, and in which sentiment and fancy are in every way so much more active than reason, the educated and uneducated are reduced to a level. We will give a large collection of omens, with their interpretation, having selected from all the best works on the subject, and will begin with "Good and Evil Days":—

1. In an old MS., the writer, after stating that the most learned mathematicians have decided that the 1st of August, the 4th of September, and the 11th of March are most injudicious to let blood, and that philosophers have settled that the 10th of August, 1st of December, and 6th of April are perilous to those who surfeit themselves in eating and drinking, continues as follows, assigning reasons why certain days should be marked as infelicitous:—

"We read of an old Arabian philosopher, a man of divers rare observations, who did remark three Mundayes in a year to be most unfortunate either to let blood or begin any notable worke, viz., the first Munday of April, ye wch day Caine was borne, and his brother Abell slaine; the 2d is the first Munday of August, the which day Sodom and Gomorrha were confounded; the 3d is the last Munday of December, the which day Judas Iscariott was borne, who betrayed our Saviour Jesus Christ. These three dayes, together with the Innocents' Day, by divers of the learned are reputed to be most unfortunate of all dayes, and ought to be eschewed by all men for ye great mishaps which often do occur in them.

"And thus much concerning the opinion of our ancient of dayes. So in like manner I will repeat unto you certain dayes yt be observed by some old writers, chiefly the ancient astrologians, who did allege that there were 28 dayes in the yeare which were revealed by the Angel Gabriel to the good Joseph, which ever have been remarked to be very fortunate dayes either to purge, let bloud, cure wounds, use marchandises, sow seed, plant trees, build houses, or taking journies, in long or short voyages, in fighting or giving of battaile, or skirmishing. They also doe alledge that children who were borne in any of these days could never be poore; and all children who were put to schooles or colledges in those dayes should become great schollars, and those who were put to any craft or trade in such dayes should become perfect artificers and rich, and such as were put to trade in marchandise should become most wealthy. The dayes be these: the 3d and 13th of January, ye 5th and 28th of

Feb., ye 3d, 22d, and 30th of March, the 5th, 22d, and 29th of April, ye 4th and 28th of May, ye 3d and 8th of June, the 12th, 18th, and 15th of July, ye 12th of August, ye 1st, 7th, 24th, and 28th of Septembr, the 4th and 15th of Octobr, ye 13th and 19th of Novr, ye 23d and 26th of December. And thus much concerning ye dayes which are by ye most curious part of ye learned remarked to bo good and evill."

2. In the *Book of Knowledge*, we find the following Evil Days:—
"Astronomers say that six days of the year are perilous of death; and therefore they forbid men to let blood of them, or take any drink; that is to say, Jan. 3, July 1, October 2, the last of April, August 4, the last day going out of December. These six days with great diligence ought to be kept, but namely [? mainly] the latter three, for all the veins are then full. For then, whether man or beast be knit in them within seven days, or certainly within fourteen days, he shall die. And if they take any drinks within fifteen days, they shall die; and if they eat any goose in these three days, within forty days they shall die; and if any child be born in these three latter days, they shall die a wicked death. Astronomers and astrologers say that in the beginning of March, the seventh night, or the fourteenth day, let the blood of the right arm; and in the beginning of April, the 11th day, of the left arm; and in the end of May, 3d or 5th day, on whether arm thou wilt; and thus, of all the year, thou shalt orderly be kept from the fever, the falling gout, the sister gout, and loss of thy sight.'

3. *A Book of Presidents* (precedents), published in London in 1616, contains a Calendar, many of the days in which have the letter B affixed: "which signifieth such dayes as the Egyptians note to be dangerous to begin or take any thing in hand, as to take a journey or any such like thing." The days thus marked are—

January 1, 2, 4, 5, 10, 15, 17, 19.
February 7, 10, 17, 27, 28.
March 15, 16, 28.
April 7, 10, 16, 20, 21.
May 7, 15, 20.
June 4, 10, 22.
July 15, 20.
August 1, 19, 20, 29, 30.
September 3, 4, 6, 7, 21, 22.
October 4, 16, 24.
November 5, 6, 28, 29.
December 6, 7, 9, 15, 17, 22.

4. May has its fatalities: the notion that to be married in it is a bad omen is as old as the age of Ovid. This is not disregarded in

the present day, which will explain the great number of marriages that take place late in April.

It is remarkable that among the thirty-three sovereigns who have sat on the English throne since William the Conqueror, although each of the eleven months has witnessed the accession of one or more, the month of May has not been so fortunate—none having ascended the throne within its limits.

5. Friday is not now generally considered an unlucky day, although many still hesitate before starting on a journey or getting married on Friday. The following facts, derived from history, show how little we have to dread " the fatal day ":

"On Friday, August 21, 1492, Christopher Columbus sailed on his great voyage of discovery. On Friday, October 12, 1492, he first discovered land. On Friday, January 4, 1493, he sailed on his return to Spain, which, if he had not reached in safety, the happy result would never have been known which led to the settlement on this vast continent. On Friday, March 15, 1493, he arrived at Palos in safety. On Friday, November 22, 1493, he arrived at Hispaniola, in his second voyage to America. On Friday, June 13, 1494, he, though unknown to himself, discovered the continent of America. On Friday, March 5, 1496, Henry VIII. of England gave to John Cabot his commission, which led to the discovery of North America. This is the first American state-paper in England. On Friday, September 7, 1565, Melendez founded St. Augustine, the oldest town in the United States by more than forty years. On Friday, November 10, 1620, the *May-Flower*, with the Pilgrims, made the harbor of Province Town, and on the same day they signed that august compact, the forerunner of our present glorious constitution. On Friday, December 22, 1620, the Pilgrims made their final landing at Plymouth Rock. On Friday, February 22, George Washington, the father of American freedom, was born. On Friday, June 16, Bunker Hill was seized and fortified. On Friday, October 7, 1777, the surrender of Saratoga was made, which had such power and influence in inducing France to declare for our cause. On Friday, September 22, 1780, the treason of Arnold was laid bare, which saved us from destruction. On Friday, October 19, 1781, the surrender at Yorktown, the crowning glory of the American arms, occurred. On Friday, July 7, 1776, the motion in Congress was made by John Adams, seconded by Richard Henry Lee, that the United States colonies were, and of right ought to be, free and independent."

6. The ancients thought that some hours in the day were fatal to life, and modern testimony corroborates this theory.

A writer in the *Quarterly Review*, having ascertained the hour of death in 2,880 instances of all ages, has arrived at this conclusion: " The *maximum* of death is from 5 to 6 o'clock A. M., when it is 40 per cent. above the average; the next, during the hour before midnight, when it is 25 per cent. in excess; a third hour of excess is that from 9 to 10 o'clock in the morning, being 17¼ per cent. above. From 10 A. M. to 3 P. M. the deaths are less numerous, being 16¼ per cent. below the average, the hour before noon being the most fatal. From 3 o'clock P. M. to 7 P. M. the deaths rise to 5¼ per cent. above the average, and then fall from that hour to 11 P. M., averaging 6¼ per cent. below the mean. During the hours from 9 to 11 o'clock in the evening there is a *minimum* of 6¼ per cent. below the average. Thus the least mortality is during midday hours, namely, from 10 to 3 o'clock; the greatest during early morning hours, from 3 to 6 o'clock."

7. "Nail gifts" are white specks on the finger-nails; which, according to their respective situations, are believed to predict certain events, as indicated in the following couplet, which is repeated whilst touching the thumb and each finger in succession:—

> A gift, a friend, a foe,
> A lover to come, a journey to go.

Sometimes the augury is expressed in positive terms; as,

> A gift on the thumb is sure to come:
> A gift on the finger is sure to linger.

This mode of prognostication is of long standing. Melton, in his "Astrologaster," a very old work, giving a catalogue of many superstitious ceremonies, tells us that "to have yellow speckles on the nailes of one's hands is a greate signe of death." In Reed's old plays, we read:

> "When yellow spots do on your hands appear,
> Be certain then you of a corse shall hear."

8. Sneezing has been held ominous from times of the most remote antiquity.

The comet of 590 was, according to some authors, the occasion of a custom, which is extensively diffused among all the nations of Christendom. In the year of this comet a frightful plague prevailed, which was alleged to be due to its influence. While the malady was at its height, a sneezing was frequently followed by death; whence the saying, *God bless you!* with which, since that time, sneezers are saluted. St. Austin tells us that "the ancients were wont to go to bed again, if they sneezed while they put on their shoe." Aristotle says: "Sneezing from noon to midnight was good, but from night to noon unlucky."

9. "Love knots" are spells or charms, made by rustics, of the blades of the oat or wheat, and sometimes of the reed-blade. Clare, in his *Shepherd's Calendar*, thus describes the making and meaning of the knots:—

> "When I was young, and went a-weeding wheat,
> We used to make them on our dinner-seat.
> We laid two blades across, and lapt them round,
> Thinking of those we loved; and, if we found
> Them linked together when unlapt again,
> Our loves were true; if not, the wish was vain.
> I've heard old women, who first told it me,
> Vow that a truer token could not be."

10. Burton notes, that when at his father's house at Lindley, in Leicestershire, he "first observed an amulet of a spider in a nut-shell, wrapped in silk, so applied for an ague" by his mother; and his surprise disappeared when he found "this very medicine in Dioscorides, approved by Matthiolus, repeated by Aldrovandus."

Ashmole says, in his *Diary:* "I took early in the morning a good dose of elixir, and hung three spiders about my neck, and they drove my ague away. Deo gratias!"—"Spiders and their webs," says Pettigrew, "have often been recommended for the cure of the ague."

11. The custom of throwing an old shoe for good luck over or after the bride and bridegroom, upon their leaving the church, or the home of the bride, after the wedding, has, of late years, been as it were revived. It is, unquestionably, one of those demonstrations of good wishes which find their way in the commonest modes of expression. But, it is not confined to weddings; the propitiation extends to all prospective views of good fortune.

It is related that an English cattle-dealer desired his wife to "trull her left shoe arter him," when he started for Norwich to buy a lottery-ticket. As he drove off on his errand, he looked round to see if she practiced the charm, and consequently he received the shoe in his face, with such force as to black his eyes. He went, and bought his ticket, which turned up a prize of 600*l*.

In Tennyson's *Lyrical Monologue* we read:

> "For this thou shalt from all things seek
> Marrow of mirth and laughter;
> And whereso'er thou move, Good Luck
> Shall throw her old shoe after."

12. The horse-shoe has been, from time immemorial, considered a protection from witchcraft and other ills; and has been nailed at the entrance of dwellings, to prevent the entrance of witches.

Butler, in "Hudibras," makes his conjuror chase away evil spirits by the horse-shoe; and Gay, in one of his Fables, makes a supposed witch complain:

> "The horse-shoe's nailed, each threshold's guard."

Nelson, the great English admiral, was of a credulous turn, had great faith in the luck of a horse-shoe, and one was nailed to the mast of the ship *Victory*. "Lucky Dr. James" attributed the success of his fever-powder to his finding a horse-shoe. When a poor apothecary, he was introduced to Newbery, of St. Paul's Churchyard, to vend the medicine for him. One Sunday morning, as James was on his way to Newbery's country-house at Vauxhall, in passing over Westminster Bridge, seeing a horse-shoe lying in the road, and considering it to be a sign of good luck, he put the shoe into his pocket. As Newbery was a shrewd man, he became James's agent for the sale of the fever-powder; whilst the doctor ascribed all his success to the horse-shoe, which he subsequently adopted as the crest upon his carriage (See 66.)

13. Cauls are little membranes found on some children, encompassing the head, when born. This is thought a good omen to the child itself, and many believe that whoever obtains it by purchase will be fortunate and escape dangers. The caul is esteemed an infallible preservative against drowning, and is much sought after by sailors. (See 75.)

14. Salt falling toward a person was considered formerly as a very unlucky omen. Something had either already happened to one of the family, or was shortly to befall the persons spilling it. It denotes also the quarreling of friends. It is thought, however, that the evil consequences arising from spilling salt may be averted by throwing a little of the salt over the left shoulder, or immediately eating a *pinch* of it. In the "British Apollo," published in London, 1708, we find the following in relation to the superstition:—

> "We'll tell you the reason
> Why spilling of salt
> Is esteemed such a fault;
> Because it doth ev'ry thing season.
> The antiques did opine,
> 'Twas of friendship a sign,
> So served it to guests in decorum;
> And thought love decayed,
> When the negligent maid
> Let the saltcellar tumble before them."

15. The casual putting the left shoe on the right foot, or the right on the left, was thought in old times to be the forerunner of some unlucky accident. Scott, in his "Discovery of Witchcraft," tells us: "He that receiveth a mischance will consider whether he put not on his shirt wrong side outwards, or his left shoe on his right foot." Thus Butler in his "Hudibras":

> "Augustus, having b' oversight,
> Put on his left shoe 'fore his right,
> Had like to have been slain that day,
> By soldiers mutin'yng for pay."

Similar to this is putting on one stocking with the wrong side outward, without design; though changing it alters the luck; and

If you accidentally put on any garment wrong side out, and make a wish before changing it, the wish will come true.

16. To arise on the *right* side is accounted lucky. In the old play of the "Dumb Knight," published 1633, Act iv., Scene 1, Alphonso says:

> "Sure I said my prayers, *rose on my right side*,
> Washed my hands and eyes, put on my girdle last;
> Sure I met no splay-footed baker,
> No hare did cross me, nor no bearded witch,
> Nor other ominous sign." (See 31.)

17. When the nose itches, it is a sign that you will have company visit you the same day. So in Dekker's old play of the "Honest Whore," Bellefront says:

"We shall ha' guests to-day, I'll lay my little maidenhead, *my nose itcheth so.*"

The reply made by her servant, Roger, further informs us that the biting of fleas was a token of the same kind. In Melton's "Astrologaster," No. 31, it is observed "that when a *man's nose itcheth* it is a sign he shall drink wine;" and in No. 32, that, "if *your lips itch*, it is a sign you shall kisse somebody."

18. The nose falling a-bleeding appears, by the following passage from an old play, to have been an omen of bad luck:—

> "How superstitiously we mind our evils!
> The throwing down of salt, or crossing of a hare,
> *Bleeding at nose*, the stumbling of a horse,
> Or singing of a cricket, are of power
> To daunt whole man in us." (See 31, 44, and 76.)

19. Washing the hands, says Grose, in the same basin, or with the same water, that another person has washed in, is extremely unlucky, as the parties will infallibly quarrel.

20. Candle omens are very numerous. Milton, in his "Astrologaster," says: "If a candle burne blue, it is a signe that there is a spirit in the house, or not farre from it." A collection of tallow, says Grose, rising up against the wick of a candle, is styled a winding sheet, and deemed an omen of death in the family.

A spark at the candle, says the same author, denotes that the party opposite to it will shortly receive a letter. A kind of fungus in the candle, observes the same writer, predicts the visit of a stranger from the part of the country nearest the object. Others say it implies the arrival of a parcel. (See 63.)

Dr. Goldsmith, in his "Vicar of Wakefield," speaking of the waking dreams of his hero's daughters, says: "The girls had their omens too; they saw rings in the candles."

21. In the "Secret Memoirs of the late Mr. Duncan Campbell,"

published in London, 1732, the author says: "I have seen people who, after writing a *letter*, have prognosticated to themselves the ill success of it, if by any accident it happened to fall to the ground: others have seemed as impatient and exclaiming against their want of thought, if through haste or forgetfulness they have chanced to hold it before the fire to dry; but the mistake of a word in it is a sure omen that whatever requests it carries shall be refused."

22. If two spoons are accidentally placed in a cup or saucer at table, it signifies a wedding will soon take place in the family.

23. To have a picture drop out of its frame, or to have a precious stone or any ornament drop from its setting while wearing or using it, is a bad omen.

Stow, in his *Chronicle*, relates that the silver cross which was wont to be carried before Wolsey fell out of its socket, and was like to have knocked out the brains of one of his servants. A very little while after came in a messenger, and arrested the Cardinal before he could get out of the house

24. The removal of a long-worn ring from the finger was thought unlucky in Elizabeth's time; for the Queen, in her last illness (says Baker), commanded the ring to be filed off her finger, wherewith she was so solemnly at first inaugurated into the kingdom, and since that time had never taken it off; it being grown into the flesh of the finger in such a manner that it could not be drawn off without filing.

25. There is an omen called "Setting the New Year in,"—that if the kindly office is performed by some one with *dark* hair, good fortune will smile on the household; while it augurs ill if a *light-haired* person is the first to enter the house in the New Year.

26. It is a very ancient superstition that all sudden pains of the body, and other sensations which could not naturally be accounted for, were presages of somewhat that was shortly to happen. Shakspeare alludes to this in the following lines from Macbeth:

> "By the pricking of my thumbs,
> Something wicked this way comes."

27. In olden times, the cat sneezing appears to have been considered as a lucky omen to a bride who was to be married the next day.

28. Small spiders, termed *money spinners*, are held by many to prognosticate good luck, if they are not destroyed or injured, or removed from the person on whom they are first observed. In the "Secret Memoirs" of Mr. Duncan Campbell, in the chapter of omens,

we read that "others have thought themselves secure of receiving money, if by chance a little spider fell upon their clothes." (See 37.)

29. It is extremely unlucky, says Grose, to kill a lady-bug, a swallow, robin redbreast, or wren. There is a particular distich, he adds, in favor of the robin and wren:

> "A robin and a wren
> Are God Almighty's cock and hen."

Persons killing any of the above-named birds or insects, or destroying their nests, will infallibly, within the course of the year, break a bone, or meet with some other dreadful misfortune. On the contrary, it is deemed lucky to have swallows build their nests in the eaves of a house, or in the chimneys.

In an old pastoral published in London, 1770, the following occurs:—

> "I found a *robin's nest* within our shed,
> And in the barn a *wren* had young one's bred.
> I never take away their nest, nor try
> To catch the old ones, lest a friend should die.
> Dick took a wren's nest from his cottage side,
> And ere a twelvemonth past his mother dy'd."

30. It is deemed very unlucky to hear a screech-owl at night. "If an owl," says Bourne, "which is reckoned a most abominable and unlucky bird, send forth its hoarse and dismal voice, it is the omen of the approach of some terrible thing—that some dire calamity and some great misfortune is at hand." (See 60.)

This omen occurs in Chaucer:

> "The jelous swan, ayenst hys deth that singeth,
> The *oule* eke, that of deth the bode bringeth."

The following lines occur in the old pastoral before quoted in 29:—

> "Within my cot, where quiet gave me rest,
> Let the dread screech-owl build her hated nest,
> And from my window o'er the country send
> Her midnight screams to bode my latter end."

31. It has always been considered a very bad omen to have a hare (see 18), sow, or weasel cross your path when going on a journey or to business. Melton, in his "Astrologaster," says, that "it is a very unfortunate thing for a man to meete early in the morning an ill-favoured man or woman, a rough-footed hen, a shag-haired dog, or a black cat." Shaw, in his "History of Money," tells us that the ancient Scots much regarded omens in their expeditions; an armed man or a wolf meeting them was a good omen; if a woman barefoot crossed the road before them, they seized her and fetched blood from her forehead; if a deer, fox, hare, or any kind of game appeared, and they did not kill it, it was an unlucky omen." We gather from a remarkable book, entitled "The School

master," published in London, 1583, that in the ages of chivalry it was thought unlucky to meet with a priest, if a man was going forth to war or a tournament.

The following superstitions among the Malabrians are related in Phillips's account of them, published in 1717: "It is interpreted as a very bad sign if a blind man, a Bramin, or a washerwoman meets one on the way; as also when one meets a man with an empty panel, or when one sees an oil-mill, or if a man meets us with his head uncovered, or when one hears a weeping voice, or sees a cat or fox crossing the way, or a dog running on his right hand, or when a poor man or a widow meets us on our way, or when we are called back." (See 41.)

Gaule, in his "Mag-astromancers Posed and Puzzel'd," holds it as a vain observation "to bode good or bad luck from the rising up on the right or left side (see 16); from lifting the left leg over the threshold, at first going out of doors; from the meeting of a beggar or a priest the first in a morning; the meeting of a virgin or a harlot first; the running in of a child between two friends; the justling one another at unawares; one treading upon another's toes; to meet one fasting that is lame or defective in any member; to wash in the same water with another." (See 19.)

32. To walk under a ladder portends disappointment.

33. To comb your hair after dark is also a sign of disappointment.

34. If a young lady loses her garter, it presages that she has an inconstant lover; therefore, O lady, when thou hast this ill augury, look about thee, and become the happy possessor of two strings to thy bow, or, what is the same thing—two beaus to thy string.

N. B.—Rich or very good-looking young ladies may treat the above with disdain.

35. If you sing before breakfast, it denotes that you will cry before supper.

36. To drop a dish-cloth, duster, or any cleaning cloth, signifies the arrival of one or more visitors.

37. If a spider, in weaving his web in some high place, comes downward before your face, you may look for money from some unexpected source. (See 28.)

38. If you make a rhyme involuntarily, before speaking again make a wish, and it will be fulfilled.

39. When you sleep in a strange bed, remember your dream and

tell it before breakfast. Observing these precautions, the dream will probably come to pass.

40. To break a needle while making a garment, is a sign that the owner will live to wear it out.

41. If you return after starting on a journey, it signifies bad luck. (See 31.)

42. To remove a cat, with a family when changing residence, will bring bad luck.

43. If a vacant rocking-chair is rocked violently, the next person who sits in it will be in danger of being ill within the year.

44. It is a lucky sign to have crickets in the house. Grose says it is held extremely unlucky to kill a cricket, perhaps from the idea of its being a breach of hospitality, this insect taking refuge in houses. The voice of a cricket, says the "Spectator," has struck more terror than the roaring of a lion.

The following line occurs in Dryden's and Lee's "Œdipus":

"Owls, ravens, *crickets*, seem the watch of death."

Melton says that "it is a signe of death to some in that house where crickets have been many yeares, if on a sudden they forsake the chimney." (See 18.)

45. It is said that a married person will not get rich until the wedding clothes are worn out. It is also said to be a sign that one will fail to get rich who tries to see to work between daylight and dark.

46. It is a bad omen to postpone a marriage after the time positively appointed.

47. If your right ear burns or itches, it is a sign that some absent person is speaking well of you; your left ear burning, signifies that you are being spoken ill of.

48. The superstition has become almost universal, that the ticking of a little insect called the "death-watch," presages the death of some one in the house.

"How many people have I seen in the most terrible palpitations, for months together, expecting every hour the approach of some calamity, only by a little worm, which breeds in an old wainscot, and, endeavoring to eat its way out, makes a noise like the movement of a watch!"—*Secret Memoirs of the late Mr. Duncan Campbell*, 1732.

The following witty account of this superstition, by Dean Swift, furnishes us with a charm to avert the omen:—

> ———"A wood-worm
> That lies in old wood, like a hare in her form,
> With teeth or with claws it will bite, or will scratch,
> And chambermaids christen this worm a death-watch,
> Because, like a watch, it always cries click;
> Then woe be to those in the house who are sick;
> For as sure as a gun they will give up the ghost,
> If the maggot cries click, when it scratches the post.
> But a kettle of boiling hot water injected
> Infallibly cures the timber affected;
> The omen is broken, the danger is over,
> The maggot will die, and the sick will recover."

49. If a knife, scissors, or any sharp-pointed instrument is dropped, and stands, sticking in the floor, company may be expected.

50. The right hand itching is a sign that the person will shake hands with a stranger; the left hand itching is a sign that money will be received soon.

51. If you sing during any meal, it is a sign you will soon be disappointed.

52. To cross a funeral procession is an ill omen.

53. To find a pearl in an oyster betokens good fortune.

54. To break a looking-glass foretells death. Grose tells us that "breaking a looking-glass betokens a mortality in the family, commonly the master." Bonaparte's (Napoleon I.) superstition upon this point is often recorded. "During one of his campaigns in Italy," says M. de Constant, "he broke the glass over Josephine's portrait. He never rested till the return of the courier he forthwith dispatched to assure himself of her safety, so strong was the impression of her death upon his mind."

55. To find a trefoil, or four-leaved clover, implies good luck; a five-leaved clover, bad luck. Melton, in his "Astrologaster," says that "if a man walking in the fields, finde any foure-leaved grasse, he shall, in a small while after, finde some good thing."

56. If four persons cross hands while in the act of shaking hands, it indicates that two of the party will soon be married.

57. If three unmarried persons having the same Christian name meet at table, it is a sign that one of the three will be married within a year.

58. To be startled by a snake is a sign of sickness.

59. When thirteen persons sit down together at table, it is a sign that one of the party will die within a year. Fosbroke, in his *Encyclopædia of Antiquities*, states that "thirteen in company was considered an unlucky number by the ancient Romans;" but he does not give any classical authority for this statement.

There is at Dantzic a clock, which at 12 admits, through a door, Christ and the eleven, shutting out Judas, who is admitted at 1. But is not the belief older than the clock? The iniquity of Judas may have led him to be considered the thirteenth at the Lord's Supper; and his self-destruction may have given to the number thirteen its fatal association.

It has, however, been explained away by M. Quetelet, in his work on *Probabilities*, as follows: "If the probability be required, that out of thirteen persons, of different ages, one of them, at least, shall die within a year, it will be found that the chances are about one to one that one death, at least, will occur. This calculation, by means of a false interpretation, has given rise to the prejudice, no less ridiculous, that the danger will be avoided by inviting a greater number of guests, which can only have the effect of augmenting the probability of the event so much apprehended."

This belief obtains in Italy and Russia, as well as in England. Moore, in his *Diary*, vol. ii., p. 206, mentions there being thirteen at dinner, one day, at Madame Catalani's, when a French countess who lived with her upstairs was sent for to remedy the grievance.

"Lord L (ansdowne) said he had dined once abroad with Count Orloff, and perceived he did not sit down at dinner, but kept walking from chair to chair; he found afterward it was because the Narishken were at table, who, he knew, would rise instantly if they perceived the number thirteen, which Orloff would have made by sitting down himself." (See 67.)

60. If a dog bays under your window at night, it portends sickness or death.

Shakspeare ranks this among omens. In the play of Henry VI., he says:—

"The owl shrieked at thy birth; an evil sign!
The night-crow cry'd, aboding luckless time;
Dogs howl'd, and hideous tempests shook down trees."

61. The howling of dogs, says Grose, is a certain sign that some one of the family will very shortly die.

The following passage is in the "Merry Devil" of Edmonton, 1631:—

"I hear the watchful dogs
With hollow howling tell of thy approach."

62. If you break your shoe-string, look out for your sweetheart, for she will bestow her love upon a stranger.

63. A flake of soot hanging at the bars of the grate, denotes the visit of a stranger, like the fungus of a candle, from the part of the country nearest the object.

Dr. Goldsmith, in his "Vicar of Wakefield," among the omens of his hero's daughters, tells us "purses bounded from the fire." In some parts of England, the cinders that bound from the fire are carefully examined by old women and children, and according to their respective forms are called either *coffins* or *purses;* and consequently thought to be presages of death or wealth.

A coal, says Grose, in the shape of a coffin, flying out of the fire towards any particular person, betokens their death not far off.

Cowper alludes to this superstition in the following lines in his "Winter Evening":—

> "Me oft has fancy, ludicrous and wild,
> Sooth'd with a waking dream of *houses, towers,*
> *Trees, churches,* and strange visages express'd
> *In the red cinders,* while with poring eye
> I gazed, myself creating what I saw.
> Nor less amused have I quiescent watch'd
> *The sooty films that play upon the bars,*
> *Pendulous, and foreboding* in the view
> Of superstition, *prophesying still,*
> Though still deceived, some stranger's near approach.

64. To drop a slice of bread, with the buttered side down, is a sign that a visitor will come hungry.

65. To eat up all the food which is on the table at tea-time, is a sign that the morrow will be a fair day.

66. In olden times it was not considered a good omen to find money. Melton says that "it is a sign of ill luck to find money." We have seen superstitious people, at the present day, keep for luck any piece of money they found, but Greene, in his "Art of Cony-Catching," a very old work, tells us: "'Tis ill lucke to keep found money." Therefore it must be spent. Mason, in his "Anatomie of Sorcerie," 1612, enumerating our superstitions, mentions as one omen of good luck, "if drink be spilled upon a man; or if he find old iron." Hence it is accounted a lucky omen to find a *horse-shoe.* (See 12.)

67. The ancients thought there was luck in odd numbers. In setting a hen, says Grose, the good women hold it as an indispensable rule to put an odd number of eggs. All sorts of remedies are ordered to be taken, three, seven, or nine times. Salutes of cannon consist of an odd number. Notwithstanding these opinions in favor of odd numbers, the number thirteen is considered very ominous. (See 59.)

Seven, as an astronomical period, is known to most nations, and has been from times prior to history.

The Hebrews commemorated their seventh day, or seventh week —(Pentecost) the seventh month (commencing their *civil* year), the the seventh year (for fallowing the land), and the seven times seventh year, or jubilee.

The seven-eared wheat is the kind formerly raised in Egypt and Syria, and is often mentioned in the Bible under the name of *corn*, which meant then any sort of grain of which bread was made. Pharaoh dreamed of the seven-eared corn.

The following are a few of the many instances of this popular adoption of the number seven: Seven Champions. Seven Churches. Seven Days in a Week. Seven Days' Notice, Seven Dials. Sevenfold. Seven Hills. Seven Penitential Psalms. Seven Senses. Seven Sisters. Seven Sleepers. Seven Sons. Seventh Son of the Seventh Son. Seven times Seven a Jubilee. Seven Wise Men. Seven Wonders of the World. Seven Years, a change. Seven abominations. The seventh son was formerly considered as endowed with pre-eminent wisdom; and the seventh son of a seventh son is still thought to possess the power of healing diseases spontaneously. Finally, perfection is likened to gold seven times purified in the fire.

The influence of the number seven over the life of President Johnson is both curious and interesting. His name consists of seven letters. At 14 (twice *seven*) years of age, he became a tailor's apprentice, at which occupation he worked *seven* years, and gave it up when twenty-one (thrice *seven*) years old. In the year 1828 (four times *seven*) he became alderman of the city of Greeneville. In the year 1835 (five times *seven*) he entered the Legislature of Tennessee. In 1842 (six times *seven*) he became member of Congress. Entered the Senate at the age of 49 (seven times *seven*.)

On the 7th of March, 1862, he was appointed Military Governor of the State of Tennessee, and in 1865, aged 56 (eight times *seven*) years, he became Vice-President of the United States.

68. A knife is in all countries an unlucky present, and a pair of scissors is equally *malapropos*. It is remarkable that no Arab will take knife or scissors from the hands of any one, as it is considered very unlucky; but they require that the instrument should first be laid upon the ground, whence they readily take it up without fear.

It is, says Grose, unlucky to present a knife, scissors, razor, or any sharp or cutting instrument to one's mistress or friend, as they are apt to cut love and friendship. To avoid the ill effects of this, a pin, a penny, or some trifling recompense, must be taken in return. Thus Gay, in his second pastoral of "The Shepherd's Week":—

> " But woe is me! such presents luckless prove,
> For *knives*, they tell me, always sever love."

69. To find a knife or razor denotes ill luck and disappointment to the party.

It is unlucky, says Grose, to lay one's knife and fork crosswise; crosses and misfortunes are likely to follow.

70. To see a new moon, for the first time, over the left shoulder, is a sign of bad luck; over the right shoulder, good luck.

71. To have money in the pocket at the time a new moon is first seen, is a sign that the person will not be out of money before the next moon.

72. A strange cat coming to the house is said to bring good luck.

73. If a bee flies in a window, and about a room, it is a sign that a letter is coming from a distance containing news.

74. If a cock crows upon a door-step early in the morning, company may be expected during the day.

75. Sailors are very superstitious; they consider it ominous to whistle on shipboard, or carry a corpse in their vessel. Whistling at sea is supposed to cause increase of the wind, and is, therefore, much disliked by seamen, though sometimes they themselves practise it when there is a dead calm. The common sailors account it very unlucky to lose a water-bucket or a mop. To throw a cat overboard, or drown one at sea, is the same. Children are deemed lucky to a ship, but clergymen and priests very unlucky. (See 13.)

76. To stumble and fall while going up stairs, is a sign you will not get married during the year. "It is lucky," says Grose, " to stumble up stairs." Probably this is a jocular observation, meaning it was lucky the party did not tumble down stairs. Melton, in his "Astrologaster," says that "if a man stumbles in a morning as soon as he comes out of dores, it is a signe of ill lucke." He adds that "if a horse stumble on the highway, it is a signe of ill lucke." (See 18.) Stumbling at a grave was anciently reckoned ominous; thus Shakspeare, in "Romeo and Juliet," Act v., Scene 3, says:

"How oft to-night
Have my old feet stumbled at graves!"

77. The bottom of the foot itching is a sign that the person will walk on strange ground.

78. The knee itching is a sign that a stranger will come to the house to sleep.

79. If your *left* eye itches, it signifies that you will cry before the day is over: if your *right* eye itches, it is a sign that you will laugh, or hear some good news; also, that you will see your love.

CONCLUDING REMARKS.

The belief in omens has existed in all ages and countries, and traces of it linger even yet in the most civilized communities, in the dread, for instance, that many entertain of sitting down to table in a party of thirteen. Not a little of the philosophy of omens is contained in the Scottish proverb: "Them who follow freits, freits follow;" meaning that a fantastic belief in impending evil paralyzes the endeavor that might prevent it.

There are few omens, perhaps none, which are not universal in their authority, though every land in turn fancies them (like its proverbs) of local prescription and origin. The death-watch extends from America to Cashmere, and across India diagonally to the remotest nook of Bengal, over three thousand miles' distance from the entrance of the Indian Punjaub. A hare crossing a man's path, on starting in the morning, has been held in all countries alike to prognosticate evil in the course of that day.

ONE HUNDRED AND EIGHTY-SEVEN WEATHER OMENS.

FOR FINE AND DRY WEATHER OF LONG CONTINUANCE.

1. If the wind be north, north-west, or east, then veer to the north-east, remain there two or three days without rain, and then veer to the south without rain; and if thence it change quickly, though perhaps with a little rain, to the north-east, and remain there—such fine weather will last occasionally for two months.

2. If there be dry weather with a weak south wind for five, six, or seven days, it having previously blown strongly from the same quarter.

3. If spiders, in spinning their webs, make the terminating filaments long, we may, in proportion to their length, conclude that the weather will be serene, and continue so for ten or twelve days.

4. If there are no falling stars to be seen on a bright summer's evening, you may look for fine weather.

5. If there be a change from continued stormy or wet to clear and dry weather, at the time of new or full moon, or a short time before or after, and so remain until the second day of the new or full moon, it is likely to remain fine till the following quarter; and if it change not then, or only for a very short time, it usually lasts until the following new or full moon; and if it does not change then, or only for

a very short time, it is likely to continue fine and dry for four or five weeks.

6. If there be a change of weather at the time of the quarters, &c. (under the same circumstances as in No. 5), it will probably last for some time.

7. Spiders generally alter their webs once in 24 hours; if they do this between six and seven in the evening, there will be a fine night; if they alter their web in the morning, a fine day; if they work during rain, expect fine weather; and the more active and busy the spider is, the finer will be the weather.

8. If near the full moon there be a general mist before sunrise; or

9. If there be a sheep-sky, or white clouds driving to the north-west, it will be fine for some days.

FOR FINE WEATHER OF SHORTER DURATION.

10. If at sunrise many clouds are seen in the west, and then disappear.

11. If, before sunrise, the fields be covered with a mist.

12. If the clouds at sunrise fly to the west.

13. If at sunrise the sun be surrounded by an iris, or circle of white clouds.

14. If there be red clouds in the west at sunset, it will be fine; if they have a tint of purple, it will be very fine; or if red, bordered with black in the south-east.

15. If there be a ring or halo round the sun in bad weather.

16. If the full moon rise clear.

17. If there be clouds in the east in the evening.

18. If the wind change from south-east, south, or south-west, through the west to the north, without storm or rain.

19. If there be a change of damp air into cloudy patches, which get thinner.

20. If clouds at the same height drive up with the wind, and gradually become thinner, and descend.

21. If a layer of thin clouds drive up from the north-west under other higher clouds driving more south.

22. If many gnats are seen in spring, expect a warm autumn.

23. If gnats fly in compact bodies in the beams of the setting sun, there will be fine weather.

24. If spiders work in the morning early at their webs, there will be a fine day.

25. If spider's webs (gossamer) fly in the autumn with a south wind, expect an east wind and fine weather.

26. If bats flutter and beetles fly about, there will be a fine morrow.

27. If there be lightning without thunder, after a clear day, there will be a continuance of fair weather.

28. If the mists vanish rapidly, and do not settle upon the hills.

29. If a north wind remain steady for two or three days.

30. If it rain before sunrise, there will be a fine afternoon.

31. If a white mist, or dew, form in the evening near a river, and spread over the adjoining land, there will be fine weather.

32. If in the morning a mist rise from over low lands, it will be fine that day.

33. If owls scream during foul weather, it will change to fair.

34. If storks and cranes fly high and steadily.

35. If there be a rainbow during continued wet weather, the rain is passing from us.

36. If a rainbow disappear suddenly, it will be fair.

37. If a leech be kept in a glass jar, about three parts filled with water, and placed in a northern aspect, its motions will denote changes in the weather. Thus, if the leech lie curled up at the bottom of the jar, the weather will be fine or frosty; if it be agitated and rise to the surface of the water, there will be rain, wind, or snow; if it be much agitated, and creep entirely out of the water, expect thunder. During heavy storms, leeches often die in great numbers.

FOR CONTINUED RAINY AND SHOWERY WEATHER.

38. If there be, within four, five, or six days, two or three changes of the wind from the north through the west to the south, without much rain and wind, and thence again through the west to the north with rain and wind, expect continued showery weather.

39. If the north-west or north wind, during three, four, or more days, blow, with rain and wind, or snow, in the winter, and then pass through the west to the south, expect continued rain and showers.

40. If the garden spiders break and destroy their webs, and creep away.

41. If the air be unusually clear during rain, or a very heavy sky, provided the moon be not above the horizon.

42. If continued fine weather change to wet by full or new moon, and remain till the second day, this bad weather will probably last until the next quarter, and not change then, or only slightly, till the next new or full moon; when, if it change not, this bad weather will very probably continue four or five weeks.

43. If there be change of continued fine weather, &c., by the quarters, &c. (under the same circumstances as in 42), the bad weather may be expected to last some time.

44. When the sky, in rainy weather, is tinged with sea green, the rain will increase; if with deep blue, it will be showery.

FOR FOUL AND WET WEATHER.

45. If the sun rise pale, or pale red, or even dark blue, there will be *rain during the day.*

46. If the clouds at sunrise be red, there will be *rain the following day.*

47. If at sunrise many dark clouds are seen in the west, and remain, there will be *rain on that day.*
48. If the sun rise covered with dark-spotted cloud; *rain the same day.*
49. If in the winter there be a red sky at sunrise; *steady rain same day;* in summer, *showers and wind.*
50. If the sun set in dark heavy clouds; *rain next day;*
51. But if it rain directly; *wind the following day.*
52. If the sun set pale or purple; *rain or wind the following day,*
53. If the sun set, and there be a very red sky in the east; *wind: in the south-east, rain.*
54. If long strips of clouds drive at a slow rate high in the air, and gradually become larger, the sky having been previously clear, there will be wet.
55. If there be many falling stars on a clear evening, in the summer, there will be *thunder.*
56. If there be a change of the wind from the north-west or west, to the south-west or south, or else from the north-east or east, to the south-east or south; *wet.*
57. If the sun burn more than usual, or there be a halo round the sun during fine weather; *wet.*
58. If it rain and the sun shine; *showers.*
59. If the full moon rise pale; *wet.*
60. If the full moon rise red; *wind.*
61. If the stars appear larger, and closer, and flicker; *rain or wind.*
62. If small white clouds, with rough edges, be seen to gather together; *there will be wind.*
63. Before thunder it often begins to blow.
64. If there be a fleecy sky, unless driving north-west; *wet.*
65. If clouds, at different heights float in different directions.
66. If an assemblage of large or small clouds spread out, or become thicker and darker.
67. If clouds suddenly appear in the south.
68. If the lower clouds drive more from the south than those above.
69. If there be rain about two hours after sunrise, it will be followed by *showers.*
70. If there be a damp fog or mist, accompanied with wind; *wet.*
71. If there be a halo round the moon, in fine weather; and the larger the circle, the nearer the *rain.*
72. If the stars above 45 degrees, especially the North Star, flicker strongly and appear closer than usual, there will be *rain.*
73. If the morning be clear and sunny, in summer or autumn, there will be *rain.*
74. If the fields in the morning be covered with a heavy wet fog, it will *generally rain within two or three days.*
75. " A rainbow in the morning is the shepherd's warning."

76. If the leaves of the trees move without any perceptible wind, *rain* may be expected.

77. If there be a west and south-west wind in July and December; *much rain.*

78. If there be a north wind in April; *rain.*

79. If there be an abundance of hoar-frost; *rain.*

80. If there be in May a south-west wind; *genial showers.*

81. If mists rise and settle on the hill-tops; *rain.*

82. If the sky, after fine weather, become wavy, with small clouds; *rain.*

83. If, in winter, the clouds appear fleecy, with a very blue sky, expect *snow or cold rain.*

84. If the clouds pass in opposite directions, both currents moving *rapidly*, expect more *rain* than in Rule 68.

85. If the wind blow between north and east, or east, with clouds, for some days, and if clouds be then seen driving from the south high up, rain will follow plentifully, sometimes forty-eight hours afterward. If, after or during the rain, the wind goes to the south or south-west; better weather.

86. If there be a continuance of rain from the south, it will be scarcely ever succeeded by settled weather before the wind changes, either to the west or some point of the north.

87. If rain fall during an east wind, it may be expected to last twenty-four hours.

88. If old and rheumatic people complain of their corns and joints; and limbs once broken ache at the place of their union.

89. If the smoke from chimneys blow down; or if soot take fire more readily than usual, or fall down the chimney into the grate; *expect rain.*

90. If ditches and drains smell stronger than usual, *expect rain;* as also if tobacco smoke seems denser and more powerful.

91. If the marigold continue shut after seven in the evening; *rain.*

92. If the convolvulus and chickweed close, there will be rain.

93. If sheep, rams, and goats spring about in the meadows, and fight more than usual.

94. If asses shake their ears, bray, and rub against walls or trees.

95. If cattle leave off feeding, and chase each other in their pastures.

96. If cats lick their bodies, and wash their faces.

97. If foxes and dogs howl and bark more than usual; if dogs grow sleepy and dull; also if they eat grass.

98. If swine be restless, and grunt loudly: if they squeak and jerk up their heads, there will be much wind; whence the proverb —" Pigs can see the wind."

99. If moles cast up hills; *rain :* if through openings in the frozen turf, or through a thin covering of snow, a change to open weather may be expected.

100. If horses stretch out their necks, and sniff the air, and assemble in the corner of a field, with their heads to leeward: *rain.*
101. If rats and mice be restless and squeak much.
102. If peacocks and guinea-fowls scream, and turkeys gobble; and if quails make more noise than usual.
103. If sea-birds fly toward land, and land-birds to sea.
104. If the cock crow more than usual, and earlier.
105. If swallows fly lower than usual.
106. If the crows make a great deal of noise, and fly round and round.
107. If water-fowl scream more than usual, and plunge into the water.
108. If birds in general pick their feathers, wash themselves, and fly to their nests.
109. If cranes place their bills under their wings.
110. If bees remain in their hives, or fly but a short distance from them.
111. If fish bite more readily, and gambol near the surface of the streams or ponds.
112. If gnats, flies, &c., bite sharper than usual.
113. If worms creep out of the ground in great numbers.
114. If frogs and toads croak more than usual.
115. If the cricket sing louder than usual.
116. If woodlice run about in great number.
117. If the owl screech.*
118. If the sea-anemone shut; and according to the extent it open, so will the weather be fine, or less so.

FOR STORM.

119. If the clouds be of different heights, the sky above being grayish or dirty blue, with hardly any wind stirring; the wind, however, changing from W. to S., or sometimes to S. E., without perceptibly increasing in force.
120. If there be a clouded sky, and dark clouds driving fast (either with the wind or more from the south), under the higher clouds, violent gusts of wind.
121. If there be long points, tails, or feathers hanging from thunder or rain clouds, five, six, or more degrees above the horizon, with little wind, in summer, thunder may be expected; but the storm will be generally of short duration.
122. If there be a light blue sky, with thin, light, flying clouds, whilst the wind goes to the south without much increase in force; or a dirty-blue sky, where no clouds are to be seen; storm.

---

* As the owl is most noisy at the change of weather, and as it often happens that patients with lingering diseases die at the change of weather, so the owl, by a mistaken association of ideas, has been said to foretell death.

123. If the sun be seen double, or more times reflected in the clouds, expect a heavy storm.

124. If the sun set with a very red sky in the east, expect stormy wind.

125. If two or three rings be seen round the moon, which are spotted and spread out, expect a storm of long continuance.

126. If porpoises and whales sport about ships.

127. If sea-gulls and other birds fly inland.

128. Storms are most frequent in December, January, and February. In September, there are generally one or two storms. If it blow in the day, it generally hushes toward evening; but if it continue blowing then, it may be expected to continue. The vernal equinoctial gales are stronger than the autumnal.

FOR INCREASE OF STORM.

129. If the sky become darker, without much rain, and divide into two layers of clouds, expect sudden gusts of wind.

130. If the sun or moon be passing through the south or north, the storm having already commenced.

FOR DECREASE OF STORM.

131. The rising or setting of sun or moon, but especially of the moon.

FOR THUNDER AND HEAVY RAIN.

132. If long horizontal strips appear with two or three edges spreading out at top into feathers, and passing over the middle of other clouds, generally there will be thunder.

133. If the clouds be uniformly black, or dark gray.

134. In May and July it thunders most; in May, expect thunder with a south-west wind.

135. If there be north-east or easterly wind in the spring, after a strong increase of heat, and small clouds appear in different parts of the sky; or if the wind change from east to south at the appearance of clouds preceded by heat.

136. If a morning fog form into clouds, at different heights, which increase in size and drive in layers.

137. If clouds float at different heights and rates, but generally in opposite directions.

138. If there be many "falling stars" on a fine summer's eve.

139. If there be sheet lightning, with a clear sky, on spring, summer, and autumn evenings.

140. If the wind be hushed with sudden heat.

141. If clover contract its leaves.

142. If there be thunder in the evening, there will be much rain and showery weather.

FOR THE APPROACH OF THUNDER.

143. If an east wind blow against a dark heavy sky from the westward, the wind decreasing in force as the clouds approach.

144. If the clouds rise and twist in different directions.

145. If the birds be silent.

146. If cattle run round and collect together in the meadows.

FOR CONTINUED THUNDER SHOWERS.

147. If there be showery weather, with sunshine, and increase of heat in the spring, a thunder-storm may be expected every day, or at least every other day.

ABATEMENT OF THUNDER STORMS.

148. If the air be very dry, with clear, yet cooler weather; or if one or two following days the atmosphere be heavy, with a little damp falling.

149. With a north wind it seldom thunders; but with a south and south-west wind, often.

FOR COLDER WEATHER.

150. If the wind change to the north and north-east.

151. If the wind change, *in summer only*, to the north-west.

152. If the wind shift to the east *in summer only*.

153. If the wind shift from south to south-east *in winter*.

FOR INCREASE OF WARMTH OR HEAT.

154. If the wind shift round to the south and south-west.

155. If the wind change from east, north-east, or north, to north-west and west, *in the winter*.

156. If the wind change to the east, *in summer only*; especially if from north-east.

157. If the wind change to south-east, *especially in summer*.

FOR FROST.

158. If birds of passage arrive early from colder climates.

159. If the cold increase *whilst it snows*, as soon as it begins to freeze.

160. If the wind blow north-east *in winter*.

161. If the ice crack much, expect the frost to continue.

162. If the mole dig his hole two feet and a half deep, *expect a very severe winter*. If two feet deep, not so severe; one foot deep, a mild winter.

163. If water-fowl or sparrows make more noise than usual; also if robins approach nearer houses than usual; *frost*.

164. If there be a dark, gray sky, with a south wind.

165. If there be continued fogs.

166. If the fire burn unusually fierce and bright, in winter, there

will be frost and clear weather; if the fire burn dull, expect damp and rain.

167. It seldom freezes with a west wind, not much with a north; most with a north-east, south-east, and sometimes south wind.

FOR THAW.

168. If snow fall in flakes, which increase in size.
169. If the heat increase in the afternoon, or suddenly before twelve o'clock.
170. If clouds drive up high from the south, south-west, or west.
171. If it freeze, and the barometer fall 20 or 30 hundredths.

MISCELLANEOUS.

172. If the dew lies plentifully on the grass after a fair day, it is the sign of another. If not, and there is no wind, rain must follow.

173. A red evening portends fine weather; but if it spread too far upward from the horizon in the evening, and especially morning, it foretells wind or rain, or both.

174. Against much rain, the clouds grow bigger, and increase very fast, especially before thunder.

175. A haziness in the air, which fades the sun's light, and makes the orb appear whitish, or ill-defined—or at night, if the moon and stars grow dim, and a ring encircles the former, rain will follow.

176. When the clouds are formed like fleeces, but dense in the middle and bright toward the edges, with the sky bright, they are signs of a frost, with hail, snow, or rain.

177. If clouds form high in air, in thin white trains, like locks of wool, they portend wind, and probably rain.

178. When a general cloudiness covers the sky, and small black fragments of clouds fly underneath, they are a sure sign of rain, and probably it will be lasting.

179. If the sun's rays appear like Moses's horns—if white at setting, or shorn of his rays, or goes down into a bank of clouds in the horizon, bad weather is to be expected.

180. If the moon look pale and dim, we expect rain; if red, wind; and if of her natural color, with a clear sky, fair weather.

181. If the moon is rainy throughout, it will be clear at the change, and perhaps the rain return a few days after. If fair throughout, and rain at the change, the fair weather will probably return on the fourth or fifth day.

182. When the new moon is first seen lying flat on its back, it foretells a drought: if it is partially inclined, sufficiently so that a pail of water might be hung on the lower horn and not spill, it denotes fair weather; if it appears to stand nearly upright, it indicates rain, and is called a wet moon.

183. If a snow-storm begins at a time when the moon is young, the rising of the moon will clear the snow away.

184. If it rains while the sun is shining, it signifies rain on the following day.

185. A rainbow toward evening is a promise of clear weather, but in the morning it betokens rain.

186. The first frost of the season appears six weeks after the katydids are first heard.

187. A fog in February denotes a frost in the following May.

HYMEN'S LOTTERY.

Let each one present deposit any sum agreed on, but of course some trifle; put a complete pack of fifty-two cards, well shuffled, in a bag or reticule. Let the party stand in a circle, and, the bag being handed around, each draw three cards. Pairs of any are favorable omens of some good fortune about to occur to the party, and gets back from the pool the sum that each agreed to pay. The king of hearts is here made the god of love, and claims double, and gives a faithful swain to the fair one who has the good fortune to draw him; if Venus, the queen of hearts, is with him, it is the conquering prize, and clears the pool; fives and nines are reckoned crosses and misfortunes, and pay a forfeit of the sum agreed on to the pool, besides the usual stipend at each new game; three nines at one draw shows the lady will be an old maid; three fives, a bad husband.

NAPOLEON'S ORACULUM; OR, BOOK OF FATE.

The Oraculum is gifted with every requisite variety of response to the following questions:

1. Shall I obtain my wish?
2. Shall I have success in my undertakings?
3. Shall I gain or lose in my cause?
4. Shall I have to live in foreign parts?
5. Will the stranger return?
6. Shall I recover my property?
7. Will my friend be true?
8. Shall I have to travel?
9. Does the person love and regard me?
10. Will the marriage be prosperous?
11. What sort of a wife, or husband, shall I have?
12. Will she have a son or daughter?
13. Will the patient recover?
14. Will the prisoner be released?
15. Shall I be lucky or unlucky?
16. What does my dream signify?

HOW TO WORK THE ORACULUM.

MAKE marks in four lines, one under another, in the following manner, making more or less in each line, according to your fancy:—

Then reckon the number of marks in each line, and, if it be *odd*, mark down one dot; if *even*, two dots. If there be more than nine marks, reckon the surplus ones over that number only, viz.:—

The number of marks in the first line of the foregoing are *odd*; therefore make one mark, thus . . . . . *
In the second, *even*, so make two, thus . . . . * *
In the third, *odd* again, make one mark only . . *
In the fourth, *even* again, two marks . . . * *

TO OBTAIN THE ANSWER.

You must refer to THE ORACULUM, at the top of which you will find a row of dots similar to those you have produced, and a column of figures corresponding with those prefixed to the questions; guide your eye down the column at the top of which you find the dots resembling your own, till you come to the letter on a line with the number of the question you are trying, then refer to the page having that letter at the top, and, on a line with the dots which are similar to your own, you will find your *answer*.

The following are unlucky days, on which none of the questions should be worked, or any enterprise undertaken: Jan. 1, 2, 4, 6, 10, 20, 22; Feb. 6, 17, 28; Mar. 24, 26; April 10, 27, 28; May 7, 8; June 27; July 17, 21; Aug. 20, 22; Sept. 5, 30; Oct. 6; Nov. 3, 29; Dec. 6, 10, 15.

** It is not right to try a question twice in one day.

ORACULUM.

Numb.	QUESTIONS.	* * * *	* * * *	** * ** *	** ** ** *	* ** * **	* * ** *	* ** * *	* * * **	** ** * *	Numb.
1	Shall I obtain my wish?	A	B	C	D	E	F	G	H	Q	1
2	Shall I have success in my undertakings?	B	C	D	E	F	G	H	I	A	2
3	Shall I gain or lose in my cause?	C	D	E	F	G	H	I	K	B	3
4	Shall I have to live in foreign parts?	D	E	F	G	H	I	K	L	C	4
5	Will the stranger return from abroad?	E	F	G	H	I	K	L	M	D	5
6	Shall I recover my property stolen?	F	G	H	I	K	L	M	N	E	6
7	Will my friend be true in his dealings?	G	H	I	K	L	M	N	O	F	7
8	Shall I have to travel?	H	I	K	L	M	N	O	P	G	8
9	Does the person love and regard me?	I	K	L	M	N	O	P	Q	H	9
10	Will the marriage be prosperous?	K	L	M	N	O	P	Q	A	I	10
11	What sort of wife or husb. shall I have?	L	M	N	O	P	Q	A	B	K	11
12	Will she have a son or a daughter?	M	N	O	P	Q	A	B	C	L	12
13	Will the patient recover from his illness?	N	O	P	Q	A	B	C	D	M	13
14	Will the prisoner be released?	O	P	Q	A	B	C	D	E	N	14
15	Shall I be lucky or unlucky this day?	P	Q	A	B	C	D	E	F	O	15
16	What does my dream signify?	Q	A	B	C	D	E	F	G	P	16

A.

‡	What you wish for, you will shortly OBTAIN.
⁂	Signifies trouble and sorrow.
⁂	Be very cautious what you do THIS day, lest trouble befall you.
⁂	The prisoner DIES, and is regretted by his friends.
⁂	Life will be spared THIS time, to prepare for death.
⁂	A very handsome daughter, but a PAINFUL one.
⁂	You will have a virtuous woman or man, for your wife or husband.
⁂	If you marry this person, you will have enemies where you little expect.
⁂	You had better decline THIS love, for it is neither constant nor true.
⁂	DECLINE your travels, for they will not be to your advantage.
⁂	There is a true and sincere friendship between you BOTH.
⁂	You will NOT recover the stolen property.
⁂	The stranger WILL, with joy, soon return.
⁂	You will NOT remove from where you are at present.
⁂	Providence WILL support you in a good cause.
⁂	You are NOT lucky.

B.

⁂	The luck that is ordained for you will be coveted by others.
⁂	Whatever your desires are, for the present decline them.
⁂	Signifies a favor or kindness from some person.
⁂	There ARE enemies who would defraud and render you unhappy.
⁂	With great difficulty he will obtain pardon or release again.
⁂	The patient should be prepared to LEAVE this world.
⁂	She will have a SON, who will be learned and wise.
⁂	A RICH partner is ordained for you.
⁂	By THIS marriage you will have great luck and prosperity.
⁂	THIS love comes from an upright and sincere heart
⁂	A higher Power WILL surely travel with you, and bless you.
⁂	Beware of friends who are false and deceitful.
⁂	You WILL recover your property—unexpectedly.
⁂	Love prevents his return home at present.
⁂	Your stay is NOT here; be therefore prepared for a change.
⁂	You will have NO GAIN; therefore be wise and careful.

C.

	With the blessing of God, you WILL have great gain.
	Very unlucky indeed—pray for assistance.
	If your desires are NOT extravagant, they will be granted.
	Signifies peace and plenty between friends.
	Be well prepared THIS day, or you may meet with trouble.
	The prisoner WILL find it difficult to obtain his pardon or release.
	The patient WILL YET enjoy health and prosperity.
	She WILL have a daughter, and will require attention.
	The person has NOT a great fortune, but is in middling circumstances.
	Decline THIS marriage, or else you may be sorry.
	Decline a courtship which MAY be your destruction.
	Your travels are IN VAIN; you had better stay at home.
	You MAY depend on a true and sincere friendship.
	You must NOT expect to regain that which you have lost.
	SICKNESS prevents the traveler from seeing you.
	It WILL be your fate to stay where you now are.

D.

	You WILL obtain a great fortune in another country.
	By venturing freely, you WILL certainly gain doubly.
	A higher Power WILL change your misfortune into success and happiness.
	Alter your intentions, or else you MAY meet poverty and distress.
	Signifies you have many impediments in accomplishing your pursuits.
	Whatever may possess your inclinations this day, abandon them.
	The prisoner WILL get free again this time.
	The patient's illness WILL be lingering and doubtful.
	She will have a dutiful and handsome son.
	The person will be LOW in circumstances, but honest-hearted.
	A marriage which WILL ADD to your welfare and prosperity.
	You love a person who does not speak well of you.
	Your travels WILL be prosperous, if guided by prudence.
	He means NOT what he says, for his heart is false.
	With some trouble and expense, you may regain your property.
	You must NOT expect to see the stranger again.

E.

⁝	The stranger WILL not return so soon as you expect.
⁝⁝	Remain among your friends, and you will do well.
⁝⁝	You will hereafter GAIN what you seek.
⁝⁝	You have NO LUCK—pray, and strive honestly.
⁝⁝	You will obtain your wishes by means of a friend.
⁝⁝	Signifies you have enemies who will endeavor to ruin you.
⁝⁝	Beware—an enemy is endeavoring to bring you to strife and misfortune.
⁝⁝	The prisoner's sorrow and anxiety are great, and his release uncertain.
⁝⁝	The patient WILL soon recover—there is no danger.
⁝⁝	She will have a daughter, who will be honored and respected.
⁝⁝	Your partner WILL be fond of liquor, and will debase himself thereby.
⁝⁝	This marriage will bring you to poverty, be therefore discreet.
⁝⁝	Their love is false to you, and true to others.
⁝⁝	DECLINE your travels for the present, for they will be dangerous.
⁝⁝	THIS person is serious and true, and deserves to be respected.
⁝⁝	You will not recover the property you have lost.

F.

	By persevering you WILL recover your property again.
	It is out of the stranger's power to return.
	You will GAIN, and be successful in foreign parts.
	A great fortune is ordained for you; wait patiently.
	There is great hindrance to your success at present.
	Your wishes are in VAIN at present.
	Signifies there are sorrow and danger before you.
	THIS day is unlucky; therefore, alter your intention.
	The prisoner will be restored to liberty and freedom.
	The patient's recovery is doubtful.
	She will have a very fine BOY.
	A worthy person, and a fine fortune.
	Your intentions would destroy your rest and peace.
	THIS love is true and constant; forsake it not.
	PROCEED on your journey, and you will not have cause to repent it.
	If you trust THIS friend, you may have cause for sorrow.

G.

✲✲✲	This friend exceeds all others in every respect.
✲✲✲	You must bear your loss with fortitude.
✲✲✲	The stranger will return unexpectedly.
✲✲✲	Remain at HOME with your friends, and you will escape misfortunes.
✲✲✲	You will meet no GAIN in your pursuits.
✲✲✲	Heaven will bestow its blessings on you.
✲✲✲	No.
✲✲✲	Signifies that you will shortly be out of the POWER of your enemies.
✲✲✲	ILL-LUCK awaits you—it will be difficult for you to escape it.
✲✲✲	The prisoner will be RELEASED by death only
✲✲✲	By the blessing of God, the patient WILL recover.
✲✲✲	A daughter, but of a very sickly constitution.
✲✲✲	You will get an honest, young, and handsome partner.
✲✲✲	Decline this marriage, else it may be to your sorrow.
✲✲✲	Avoid this love.
✲✲✲	Prepare for a short journey; you will be recalled by unexpected events.

H.

	Commence your travels, and they will go on as you could wish.
	Your pretended friend hates you secretly.
	Your hopes to recover your property are vain.
	A certain affair prevents the stranger's return immediately.
	Your fortune you will find in abundance abroad.
	Decline the pursuit, and you will do well.
	Your expectations are vain—you will not succeed.
	You will obtain what you wish for.
	Signifies that on this day your fortune will change for the better
	Cheer up your spirits, your luck is at hand.
	After LONG imprisonment, he will be released.
	The patient will be relieved from sickness.
	She will have a healthy SON.
	You will be married to your equal in a short time.
	If you wish to be happy, do not marry this person.
	This love is from the heart, and will continue until death.

I.

	The love is great, but will cause great jealousy.
	It will be in vain for you to travel.
	Your friend will be as sincere as you could wish him to be.
	You will recover the stolen property through a cunning person.
	The traveler will soon return with joy.
	You will not be prosperous or fortunate in foreign parts.
	Place your trust in God, who is the disposer of happiness.
	Your fortune will shortly be changed into misfortune.
	You will succeed as you desire.
	Signifies that the misfortune which threatens will be prevented.
	Beware of your enemies, who seek to do you harm.
	After a short time, your anxiety for the prisoner will cease.
	God will give the patient health and strength again.
	She will have a very fine daughter.
	You will marry a person with whom you will have little comfort.
	The marriage will not answer your expectations.

K.

	After much misfortune, you will be comfortable and happy.
	A sincere love from an upright heart.
	You will be prosperous in your journey.
	Do not RELY on the friendship of this person.
	The property is lost for EVER; but the thief will be punished.
	The traveler will be absent some considerable time.
	You will meet luck and happiness in a foreign country.
	You will not have any success for the present.
	You will succeed in your undertaking.
	Change your intentions, and you will do well.
	Signifies that there are rogues at hand.
	Be reconciled, your circumstances will shortly mend.
	The prisoner will be released.
	The patient will depart this life.
	She will have a son.
	It will be difficult for you to get a partner.

L.

	You will get a very handsome person for your partner.
	Various misfortunes will attend this marriage.
	This love is whimsical and changeable.
	You will be unlucky in your travels.
	This person's love is just and true. You may rely on it.
	You will lose, but the thief will suffer most.
	The stranger will soon return with plenty.
	If you remain at home, you will have success.
	Your gain will be trivial.
	You will meet sorrow and trouble.
	You will succeed according to your wishes.
	Signifies that you will get money.
	In spite of enemies, you will do well.
	The prisoner will pass many days in confinement.
	The patient will recover.
	She will have a daughter.

M.

	She will have a son, who will gain wealth and honor.
	You will get a partner with great undertakings and much money.
	The marriage will be prosperous.
	She, or He, wishes to be yours this moment.
	Your journey will prove to your advantage.
	Place no great trust in that person.
	You will find your property at a certain time.
	The traveler's return is rendered doubtful by his conduct.
	You will succeed as you desire in foreign parts.
	Expect no gain; it will be in vain.
	You will have more LUCK than you expect.
	Whatever your desires are, you will speedily obtain them.
	Signifies you will be asked to a wedding.
	You will have no occasion to complain of ill-luck.
	Some one will pity and release the prisoner.
	The patient's recovery is unlikely.

N.

	The patient will recover, but his days are short.
	She will have a daughter.
	You will marry into a very respectable family.
	By this marriage you will gain nothing.
	Await the time and you will find the love great.
	Venture not from home.
	This person is a sincere friend.
	You will never recover the theft.
	The stranger will return, but not quickly.
	When abroad, keep from evil women or they will do you harm.
	You will soon gain what you little expect.
	You will have great success.
	Rejoice ever at that which is ordained for you.
	Signifies that sorrow will depart, and joy will return.
	Your luck is in blossom; it will soon be at hand.
	Death may end the imprisonment.

O.

	The prisoner will be released with joy.
	The patient's recovery is doubtful.
	She will have a son, who will live to a great age.
	You will get a virtuous partner.
	Delay not this marriage—you will meet much happiness.
	None loves you better in this world.
	You may proceed with confidence.
	Not a friend, but a secret enemy.
	You will soon recover what is stolen.
	The stranger will not return again.
	A foreign woman will greatly enhance your fortune.
	You will be cheated out of your gain.
	Your misfortunes will vanish and you will be happy.
	Your hope is in vain—fortune shuns you at present.
	That you will soon hear agreeable news.
	There are misfortunes lurking about you.

P.

*****	This day brings you an increase of happiness.
*****	The prisoner will quit the power of his enemies.
*****	The patient will recover and live long.
*****	She will have two daughters.
*****	A rich young person will be your partner.
*****	Hasten your marriage—it will bring you much happiness.
*****	The person loves you sincerely.
*****	You will not prosper from home.
*****	This friend is more valuable than gold.
*****	You will NEVER receive your goods.
*****	He is dangerously ill, and cannot yet return.
*****	Depend upon your own industry, and remain at home.
*****	Be joyful, for future prosperity is ordained for you.
*****	Depend not too much on your good luck.
*****	What you wish will be granted to you.
*****	That you should be very careful this day, lest any accident befall you.

Q.

	Signifies much joy and happiness between friends.
	This day is not very lucky, but rather the reverse.
	He will yet come to honor, although he now suffers.
	Recovery is doubtful; therefore, be prepared for the worst.
	She will have a son who will prove forward.
	A rich partner, but a bad temper.
	By wedding this person you insure your happiness.
	The person has great love for you, but wishes to conceal it.
	You may proceed on your journey without fear.
	Trust him not; he is inconstant and deceitful.
	In a very singular manner you will recover your property.
	The stranger will return very soon.
	You will dwell abroad in comfort and happiness.
	If you will deal fairly you will surely prosper.
	You will yet live in splendor and plenty.
	Make yourself contented with your PRESENT fortune.